Washington
NATIONAL FORESTS

Written by
Wendy Walker

ABOUT THE AUTHOR

Wendy Walker works as an interpretive specialist for the Mount Baker-Snoqualmie National Forest and as a regional and national consultant for Forest Service interpretive projects. She has presented training sessions on interpretive writing, planning, research skills, and programming and has taught a university course in environmental interpretation. She also works privately as an interpretive writer and project designer and has developed environmental education curriculum.

ACKNOWLEDGMENTS

Thanks to the people from each of the national forests who answered my questions, offered facts and stories, reviewed text, searched out photographs, and guided me out into the woods.

Special credit is due to Jean Claybo, who had the idea in the first place, and to Penny Falknor, for being Forest Service coordinator for the project.

And to my family — Carey, Erin, and Alden — thank you for your patience.

NATIONAL FORESTS OF AMERICA SERIES

Copyright ©1991 by Falcon Press Publishing Co., Inc., Helena and Billings, Montana

Published in cooperation with the Forest Service, U.S. Department of Agriculture

All rights reserved, including the right to reproduce this book in any form, except brief quotations for reviews, without the written permission of the publisher.

Design, typesetting and other prepress work by Falcon Press, Helena, Montana. Printed in Korea.

Library of Congress Number 91-71622

ISBN 1-56044-033-3

Front cover photo: Mount Baker, Mount Baker-Snoqualmie National Forest. LEE MANN

Back cover photos: Rainforest in the Soleduck River Valley, Olympic National Forest. KIRKENDALL / SPRING; blacktail fawn, Gifford Pinchot National Forest. ART WOLFE; whitewater rafting, Okanogan National Forest. ERIC SANFORD

Title page photo: Icicle Creek area, Wenatchee National Forest. PAT O'HARA

For additional copies of this book, please check with your local bookstore, or write to Falcon Press, P.O. Box 1718, Helena, MT 59624, or call toll free 1-800-582-2665.

FALCON® PRESS

Contents

WASHINGTON NATIONAL FORESTS

4	Introduction: Where diversity reigns
8	Olympic: Almost an island unto itself
28	Mount Baker-Snoqualmie: Escape from the city
44	Wenatchee: From glaciers to sagebrush
64	Okanogan: A land along the border
80	Gifford Pinchot: A land of volcanoes
96	Colville: An overlooked treasure
112	Kaniksu: Small in area, big in rewards
118	Umatilla: Far from the madding crowds
124	Conclusion: Meeting regional and national needs

The Norse Peak Wilderness touches parts of three national forests— the Gifford Pinchot, Mount Baker-Snoqualmie, and Wenatchee — as it straddles the Cascade crest. PAT O'HARA

Introduction

N A T I O N A L F O R E S T S

Where diversity reigns

North America has been floating westward and running aground on eastbound Pacific Ocean floor for hundreds of millions of years. Washington state has been at the prow of North America during the collision. As the huge land masses smashed into each other, the surface of the state crumpled into ridges, peaks, and highlands.

These wrinkles in the earth's crust create the mountain ranges of Washington: the Olympics in the west, Cascades near the middle, Selkirks in the northeast, and Blue Mountains in the southeast. They give the state its towering peaks, erupting volcanoes, active glaciers, cascading waterfalls, and its eight national forests.

On a map, these national forests — the Olympic, Gifford Pinchot, Mount Baker-Snoqualmie, Okanogan, Wenatchee, Colville, Kaniksu, and Umatilla — look like green patchwork fabric cut to fit the mountain ranges. Homesteaders in the late 1800s claimed the fertile lowlands, leaving steep slopes and rocky peaks to the federal government. Most of the high country remains public land today, much of it within national forest boundaries. The nine million acres of national forest in Washington make up 20 percent of the state, covering an area the size of Switzerland.

A traveler flying over the Washington national forests of today would first see the Olympic

Mountains at the western edge of the state. The range rises from the Pacific Ocean into a rugged mound of ice-capped peaks, surrounded on three sides by salt water. Slopes below timberline are in the national forest, while the ridges and peaks of the 8,000-foot mountains lie within Olympic National Park.

Farther east, the Cascade Range forms the rocky spine of Washington state, running 300 miles north-south from Canada to Oregon. Many of the jagged, glacier-carved summits reach 9,000 feet, while the snowy domes of volcanoes soar up to 14,000 feet. Three-fourths of the glaciers in the continental United States mantle the Cascades because of world-record snowfall.

The Mount Baker-Snoqualmie and Gifford Pinchot national forests blanket the western slopes of the Cascades. The Okanogan and Wenatchee national forests cover the eastern slopes. Most of the rest of the Cascade Range lies within North Cascades and Mount Rainier national parks and the Yakima Indian Reservation.

Northeast from the Cascades, Washington undulates into the Okanogan Highlands. These meadowed hills, crowned with trees, are shared by the Okanogan and Colville national forests. The state then crumples upward into the wild Selkirk Mountains in the northeastern corner. The Washington portion of these 7,000-foot mountains falls within the Colville National Forest, except for a small portion included with the Kaniksu National Forest, part of the Idaho Panhandle National Forests.

In the southeastern corner of the state lie the Blue Mountains of the Umatilla National Forest. Steep-sided streams cut through this series of lava plateaus. Washington and Oregon share both the mountain range and the national forest.

The mountains of Washington create their own weather. The western ranges specialize in snagging Pacific Ocean storms, and the eastern mountains are masters at cooking up thunderstorms.

Huge masses of clouds saturated with water boil in off the Pacific Ocean and slam into the mountain ranges during most of the year. The clouds rise and cool and drop most of their moisture on the western slopes. Clouds descending the eastern sides in the "rainshadow" often are wrung dry.

Differing climates and landforms create striking contrasts in plant and animal communities within the national forests. In one location, high on a mountain

A river otter takes refuge in a tree trunk along the Skagit River, a designated Wild and Scenic River in the Mount Baker-Snoqualmie National Forest. ART WOLFE

ridge next to a glacier cracked with deep blue crevasses, cold winds could be ruffling the fur of a mountain goat. Dark crags tower above, glistening with meltwater. Thick stands of fir and hemlock fill the river valleys below.

In the same national forest, fifty miles east and thousands of feet lower, the temperature could be forty degrees warmer and the air much drier. Tufts of sagebrush grow in steep, waterless gullies. A rattlesnake slithers onto a rocky ledge to bask in the hot sun. Breezes carry the vanilla smell of a lone ponderosa pine nearby.

Contrasting ecosystems such as these help create a stunning array of recreational opportunities in Washington's national forests, which record about 17.6 million recreation visitor days each year. The Mount Baker-Snoqualmie National Forest ranks fourth in the nation for recreation visitor days.

Climbers and hikers from around the world come to the national forests to scale rock cliffs, ascend glaciers, stroll through wildflower meadows, and wander among huge old trees. Others come to challenge themselves or seek solitude in millions of acres of wildernesses.

Rafters, canoers, and kayakers ride the rapids of the whitewater rivers. Anglers fish the rushing streams and clear, still alpine lakes. Hunters stalk deer, elk, bear, and grouse each fall. Downhill skiers swish down the runs of ski areas. Cross-country skiers and snowmobilers explore snow-covered forest roads.

Visitors also enjoy scenic drives, nature trails, ranger programs, wildlife viewing, photography, picnicking, and camping.

In addition to offering this wealth of recreational opportunities, the national forests of Washington help feed, clothe, and house the human race.

National forests differ from national parks, which were set aside purely for recreation and to preserve the land. Congress created the national forests in the late 1800s for a number of uses. Gifford Pinchot, the first chief of the Forest Service, summarized the historic role of the national forests when he said their purpose was to provide the greatest good for the greatest number of people for the longest time.

National forests in Washington contain some of the fastest-growing trees in the world. Billions of board feet of timber from these forests each year become lumber, paper, and other wood products. Timber sales on public lands provide work for loggers and mill employees, and the proceeds fill federal, state, and local treasuries.

The national forests also provide grazing land for livestock, drinking water for cities, irrigation water for farms, minerals, floral greens, medicinal plants, rocks, gravel, berries, mushrooms, firewood, and Christmas trees.

The Forest Service is the federal agency faced with the challenging responsibility of managing the national forests to meet human needs while maintaining the long-term health of ecosystems.

Typical Forest Service planning meetings might include discussions involving an ecologist, a biologist, a geologist, an archaeologist, a forester, an engineer, and a recreation planner. They all present data from their fields to help decide issues such as where timber harvest should be located, how fish habitat can be improved, or which new recreation facilities are needed. Their different points of view add depth and balance to the resulting recommendations.

Management proposals created during such team meetings are often presented to the public, so citizens can offer their ideas. When all the suggestions and information are in, land managers decide usage issues.

Perhaps the best way to learn about the national forests of Washington is to dive in and experience them. And the forests offer a myriad of experiences. Each of the following scenes could occur in a single day within a national forest of Washington.

• Morning sunlight slants through thick trunks of ancient hemlock and cedar trees. Dark green moss fattens limbs, and light green lichens hang from branches like beards. High in a tree, a small brown vole nibbles a lichen. The song of a thrush trills through the forest, and treetops rustle in the wind as berry pickers pluck fat, blue huckleberries from a bush.

• On a hillside a few miles away, a whistle toots. The smell of fresh-cut trees fills the air. A logger fastens a steel cable around a log, for hoisting it into the air and up to a landing on a gravel road. A yellow loader clasps the log in steel jaws, swivels, and lowers it on a logging truck.

• In the late afternoon, a river raft noses down a smooth tongue of water in a valley bottom and plummets into the white chaos of a rapid. Icy waves crash over the rafters inside, who paddle madly, whooping with delight.

• The sun has set. Flames leap in the firegrate of a campsite. Firelight flickers on the faces of a young boy and girl listening to their father's ghost story. An owl hoots nearby, startling the storyteller. The whole family laughs. Another day draws to a close in a national forest of Washington. ■

Tiger lilies, one of the showiest of the wildflowers, look almost as if they had been cultivated in a garden. The flowers can be found at the edges of many forested areas. PAT O'HARA

Graves Creek flows through a shaggy corridor of moisture-loving trees in the Olympic National Forest. RAY ATKESON

Olympic
NATIONAL FOREST

Almost an island unto itself

A dome of mountains swells up in the middle of the Olympic Peninsula, in the westernmost reaches of Washington state. Glaciers cap and carve the jumble of peaks at the center. Rivers run down all sides in a radiating pattern of valleys. The Olympic Mountains stand alone, unconnected to any other range. Ocean hems them in on three sides, and on the fourth side, lowlands separate them from the Cascade Range.

The Olympic National Forest runs around the waist of the Olympic Mountains like a belt. Although occasionally extending up to the mountaintops or down to sea level, most of the national forest's 632,324 acres lie on timbered ridges and in valleys from 500 to 3,500 feet above sea level. The peaks and meadows of Olympic National Park rise above the national forest. Indian reservations, state forests, and private lands spread over the lowlands below it.

The Olympic National Forest is part of a network of land management agencies on the Olympic Peninsula that cooperate in managing ecosystems that flow from one administrative area to another. For example, the Forest Service manages habitat for fish, while the fish are managed by the state Wildlife and Fisheries departments and the Indian tribes of the Olympic Peninsula.

Salmon don't notice boundaries when they swim up from the ocean, through the Quinault Indian

Reservation and into the Olympic National Forest and Olympic National Park to spawn. They care only that the river flows clear, spawning gravels are clean, and no barriers block their way.

The Quinault Indian tribe, Washington Departments of Fisheries and Wildlife, Forest Service, and National Park Service work together to meet the needs of the salmon. This may involve limits on fishing, interagency management of a fish hatchery, or tribal input on timber sales.

In a fifty-mile span from west to east, the climate on the Olympic National Forest ranges from wet, mild maritime conditions with some of the heaviest precipitation in the world to drier weather more commonly found in eastern Washington. Vegetation varies from wet forests of Sitka spruce and sword fern to dry isolated stands of lodgepole pine and even an occasional juniper tree. Between these two extremes can be found the Douglas-fir and western hemlock that make up the majority of timber stands on the national forest.

The types of animals in different areas of the national forest also vary, depending on climate, landforms, and vegetation. The Olympic provides habitat for sixty-one species of mammals, 226 bird species, seven reptile species, and fifteen amphibian species. Animals adapt to environments that meet their needs, interrelating with other animals, plants, and the physical environment to form an ecosystem.

More than 3,000 Roosevelt elk roam the national forest on the western side of the mountains. They are less likely to be found on the eastern side, because they have adapted to wet forest ecosystems on the west side. Some species native to the Olympics, such as Roosevelt elk, Olympic marmot, and Cope's salamander, have

The summit of Mount Ellinor, at 5,944 feet, offers this commanding view of the wild interior of the Olympic Mountains. Mount Ellinor rises at the eastern edge of the range in the Mount Skokomish Wilderness.
BOB AND IRA SPRING

developed distinctive characteristics due to geographic isolation. The Olympic marmot, for example, is smaller than the hoary marmot found elsewhere.

The communities at the edges of the national forest vary, as well. Towns on the west half of the Olympic tend to be small, geographically isolated, and economically dependent on national forest resources. Indians living on Olympic Peninsula reservations depend on the national forest for traditional spiritual and resource harvest activities.

Communities on the eastern side of the Olympic Peninsula are closer to the cities of Puget Sound. They are less isolated and more economically diverse. Many residents use the national forest primarily as a recreation area.

Columbine flowers, left, nod gracefully on their stalks in moist places in open forest, at the edges of clearings, and along roadsides. These members of the buttercup family are pollinated by hummingbirds.
TOM AND PAT LEESON

Roosevelt elk males spar in the fall during mating season. With branched antlers locked, the bulls push at each other in an eyeball-to-eyeball shoving match. They also rub bark off saplings with their antlers, to leave territorial messages for other bulls.
TOM AND PAT LEESON

Olympic National Forest employees face the challenge of balancing the needs of many different ecosystems with a wide array of human needs and wants. Congress mandates that the Forest Service manage resources for the benefit of people, while maintaining long-term ecosystem health.

People want wood products from the national forest, so the Forest Service sells timber to private contractors for harvest. Trees grow vigorously in the wet, mild climate and volcanic soils of the Olympic Peninsula. Foresters estimate that trees in the Olympic National Forest add enough new growth each year to build 30,000 homes. In the 1980s, an average 242.8 million board feet was cut on national forest land each year.

Planning timber harvests that maintain long-term forest health can be challenging. Information on such factors as climate, soil, water, and wildlife habitat

Old-growth treetops grow so close together that they block most sunlight from reaching the forest floor. Few plants can thrive in the dim light near the ground, allowing open park-like areas between the trees. ART WOLFE

helps determine where, when, how, and which trees to cut. Forest Service timber managers recognize that any change in an ecosystem initiates a whole chain of events that can sometimes have far-reaching consequences for animals, plants, and people.

For example, harvesting a stand of mature trees provides employment for local loggers and mill workers, money for schools, and wood products for people around the United States. Particularly straight-grained trees may become special lumber used to repair historic fishing boats. Redcedar may go to an Indian tribe for carving a racing canoe or building a traditional longhouse. Families may cut firewood from the logging debris.

People who have been camping or birdwatching in the mature grove may choose other recreational spots. But others, such as hunters, may find new opportunities as elk and deer begin foraging in the harvest area.

Two blacktail fawns pause on a hillside. When the fawns grow old enough to wander, their mother can locate them by smelling for their footprints. Deer have glands between the lobes of their hooves that deposit scent with every step.
TOM AND PAT LEESON

Indian paintbrush add fiery reds and oranges to meadows. Paintbrush are partial parasites. They have green leaves and are capable of making their own food, but attach themselves to other plants underground and steal nutrients.
SCOTT PRICE

Hikers on the Mt. Townsend trail in the Buckhorn Wilderness can walk through extravagant wild gardens of rhododendron blossoms in the late spring, top left. The hike to the 6,280-foot summit is eleven miles round trip, offering pleasant lakeside camping along the way. PAT O'HARA

Timber harvest must be planned with sensitivity to wildlife habitat needs. A large percentage of the animals in the national forest depend on the older trees for habitat. Marbled murrelets, sea birds from the Pacific that nest in the old trees, may be affected. Roosevelt elk, which use the trees for winter cover, may begin intruding on private cattle pastures. During the summer, elk may begin eating the new growth in the logged area, benefiting from the harvest.

The mature stand may have been shielding a rare grove of chinquapin trees from the wind. Without the old growth, these relatives of the oaks could blow down the next winter, and a species of butterfly that lives only on the chinquapin — the golden hairstreak — would disappear from the Olympic National Forest.

Foresters taking all these variables into account are managing ecosystems instead of crops of trees. Forest ecology research helps them plan timber harvests that minimize the effects on ecosystems. Ecologists have identified eight vegetative zones on the Olympic National Forest — six forested, one subalpine, and one alpine. The zones contain scores of plant communities.

A separate set of considerations exists for harvesting in each area, based on such factors as the rarity of plants and animals, insect and disease infestations, growth rate of trees, and likelihood of survival of seedlings. Harvest is planned for areas with high growth and revegetation rates.

Millions of seedlings are planted each year to reforest harvest areas. Much of the seed for the young trees comes from the Dennie Ahl Seed Orchard, located on the national forest near the town of Shelton. The

Clearcuts, left, after logging provide summer feeding habitat for Roosevelt elk. The elk prefer grasses that can grow only in open areas with ample sunlight. In the winter, the elk retreat to the cover of dense forests. TOM AND PAT LEESON

FORESTS THAT LOVE THE RAIN

Thick, gray clouds blanket the sky. Mist wreathes huge trees. Water drips from branches draped with lichen and moss. This is the great, wet forest of the western Olympic Peninsula.

Up to twenty feet of rain falls here each year. Thick layers of rotting wood on the forest floor hold moisture like a sponge, keeping roots damp even during dry summers. Trees thrive in the rain and fog. Sitka spruce, western hemlock, and western redcedar reach world-record sizes on the Olympic Peninsula.

This lush forest has been called the only temperate rain forest in the world. Although it shares such characteristics as dense vegetation and heavy yearly rainfall with rain forests, the Olympics are too dry in July and August to create a true rain forest. Trees that need constant moisture, such as Sitka spruce, survive the summer drought because fog drenches them on most days. Fog blows in off the Pacific Ocean, condenses on branches, and drips to the ground, adding four more feet to the yearly precipitation.

Trees in this forest are some of the largest and oldest living things on earth. They can grow up to 300 feet tall, measure sixty feet around, and live for more than 1,000 years. Fifteen hundred organisms may live on a single tree. The old giant trees owe their size and vitality to an elegant web of relationships among smaller creatures in the forest.

Fungi in the soil grow sheaths around tree roots, feeding them nutrients. Trees with fungi grow

Trees die, fall to the ground, and decay in old-growth forests, building up thick layers of rotting debris. Gardens of ferns and moss carpet these fertile natural compost heaps. KIRKENDALL/SPRING

much better than those without. The fungi never sprout above ground, so they need small mammals such as voles to help them reproduce. These rodents dig up and eat the fruiting bodies of the fungi. When the animals defecate, they spread the spores around, complete with fertilizer.

Vole populations are kept in check by such predators as flying squirrels and spotted owls. In turn, the squirrels and spotted owls feed larger predators, such as great-horned owls. When the animals die and decompose, they return nutrients to the soil, feeding the fungi and the trees.

Forests growing within the Olympic National Forest are full of connections like these. They function like giant organisms made up of a variety of essential parts. When the parts are healthy and the connections intact, a tremendous forest organism can grow, such as the world-class trees of the Olympic Peninsula.

U.S. Highway 101 in the Olympic National Forest weaves through one of the mightiest forests in the world, as it connects all four ranger stations in the national forest and offers visitors access to numerous trails and attractions. Some of the trees here reach heights of more than 200 feet. TOM AND PAT LEESON

orchard produces genetically superior seed adapted to specific environments within the Olympic National Forest. Researchers have found that trees grow best when planted in the same kind of environments as their parent trees.

Timber harvest is not the only management challenge on the Olympic National Forest. Locating trails and campgrounds, keeping wildernesses wild, maintaining wildlife habitat, and preserving cultural resources also take forethought, skill, and research. For example, proposed construction of a campground on top of a hidden archaeological site or in spotted owl habitat raises conflicting issues that must be resolved.

Forest managers must decide whether campsites or the integrity of archaeological sites is more important or whether human recreation or owl survival should have higher priority. These and other tough questions face Olympic National Forest land managers every day. Finding equitable solutions is the challenge, and citizens often have a voice in the decisions.

A good example of public involvement occurred in the late 1980s, with public response to the Olympic National Forest plan. Thousands of people attended

Mmmm, good. Huckleberries offer a refreshing break during a hike, satisfying both hunger and thirst. One low-bush species has a Latin name that fits the taste of its berries, Vaccinium deliciosum. JERRY PAVIA

People aren't the only creatures fishing in the national forest. Black bears are omnivorous opportunists, meaning they will eat almost anything. Most of their diet consists of plants, with a preference for berries in season. During salmon spawning runs, fish add a tasty variety to their meals. TOM AND PAT LEESON

public meetings and wrote letters indicating what they wanted for national forest lands. The Olympic National Forest now operates under guidelines molded by this process.

Public opinion about the Olympic National Forest has changed through time. The Cooperative Sustained Yield Unit near Shelton provides an example of a program that met the values of the 1940s but is being re-examined today.

Congress created the Cooperative Sustained Yield Unit in 1944 by combining private timber land owned by Simpson Timber Company with Olympic National Forest land, for timber management. The idea was to maintain community stability by providing a steady flow of timber to mills in the towns of Shelton and McCleary. At the time, Simpson had cut most of the mature trees on its land and was considering closing its mills. The economic survival of the local communities appeared threatened.

The cooperative agreement called for replanting Simpson lands and managing them as a reservoir of young trees for future harvest. Timber on national

Pileated woodpeckers, left, are spectacular crow-sized birds with red crests. Their chisel beaks, long tongues, and stiff tails that act as props when climbing, adapt them admirably for drilling holes in dead trees to eat insects. TOM AND PAT LEESON

Summer fog off the Pacific Ocean drenches the forests of the western Olympic Peninsula. Some plants and trees that need constant moisture survive the late summer rainless period only because of the regular fog.
BOB AND IRA SPRING

forest land could then be harvested at accelerated levels to fill the gap until the Simpson trees reached maturity. The replanted national forest land would then become the bank of young trees, and Simpson lands would again produce timber for the mills.

The cooperative agreement guaranteed Simpson the sole right to purchase any national forest timber sold from the Cooperative Sustained Yield Unit. Simpson, in return, promised to process the logs within ten miles of Shelton and McCleary. After the agreement, Simpson expanded and modernized its mills, and the local communities experienced economic stability.

As the program is re-evaluated, the question of whether the unit still meets the needs of the times will be considered. Its answer will depend partly on how societal values have changed.

Changes in society have also led to increasing recreational use of the Olympic National Forest. Urban stress, rising incomes, increased leisure time, growing populations in the Puget Sound area, and improved roads from urban centers to the Olympic Peninsula have sent an increasing number of people to the national forest for rest, relaxation, and adventure.

Recreation opportunities within the national forest include sightseeing, scenic drives, hiking, climbing, boating, fishing, hunting, berry picking, photography, and camping. The Olympic National Forest records almost two million recreation visits each year.

U.S. Highway 101 travels 340 miles around the perimeter of the Olympic Peninsula, creating a paved driving loop that connects all four ranger stations of the national forest. Each ranger station offers information and maps.

Thousands of miles of gravel side roads turn off Highway 101 and lead into the national forest. Forest roads follow river valleys and switchbacks up ridges to scenic views, trailheads, dispersed camping, and developed campgrounds. Many side trips also offer unique recreational highlights.

Those driving counter-clockwise on the Highway

A bigleaf maple tree rains its autumn leaves on the evergreen branches of a western hemlock tree, along the Duckabush River corridor. PAT O'HARA

A RESTFUL STEP INTO THE PAST

After passing miles of clearcuts and young trees, U.S. Highway 101 northbound from Aberdeen burrows suddenly into a towering old-growth forest. The change is abrupt because the road enters the Quinault Research Natural Area of the Olympic National Forest — a 1,468-acre area set aside in 1932 for scientific research and preservation of an undisturbed ecosystem.

The giant Sitka spruce, western hemlock, Douglas-fir, and western redcedar have been growing here for centuries. Most soar more than 200 feet in height, and some are twelve feet in diameter. This magnificent grove allows a glimpse of the kind of forests that once covered the western lowlands of the Olympic Peninsula.

The big trees also provide a gateway to one of the recreation highlights of the Olympic Peninsula, the Quinault Valley. Visitors who turn off the highway in the next few miles travel to Quinault Lake, a large tree-rimmed lake dammed by a gravel moraine left by Ice Age glaciers. The north and south shore roads join above the lake and follow the Quinault River into the Olympic Mountains.

The glaciers dug a big hole when they gouged the steep-sided basin now filled by Quinault Lake. Soundings indicate that the water is 100 feet deep just a few boat lengths from shore. The center of the lake is more than 200 feet deep.

The lake water is cold. Modern glaciers on the sides of 7,000-foot Mount Anderson feed the Quinault River with meltwater. Fish thrive in the cold water. Sockeye salmon make the lake their home for the one to two years of stillwater habitat they need during their early development. Other fish also live in the lake, including the rare blueback salmon.

Rays of sun slant through the trunks of old trees, splintering the shadows of the dense forest. ART WOLFE

Paths beckon Lake Quinault visitors to stroll through ancient forests.
ART WOLFE

The Quinault Indian tribe raises fish in net pens at the hatchery near the lake outlet. The tribe manages fish populations in the lake and sells tribal fishing licenses to the public at several lakeside businesses. The Quinault River below the lake is entirely on the Quinault Indian Reservation and is closed to non-Indians unless they are traveling with an Indian guide.

More than twelve feet of rain falls every year at Lake Quinault, mostly during the winter months. This extravagent moisture has helped produce some of the largest trees in the world. A Sitka spruce on private resort land near the lake is the largest such spruce in the world, at more than nineteen feet in diameter. Twelve adults holding hands, arms outstretched, could barely encircle the sixty-foot girth.

The north shore of Lake Quinault lies within Olympic National Park, while the south shore is part of the Olympic National Forest. The south shore road hugs the lake as it travels to Forest Service campgrounds, trails, a visitor information center, and private resorts and houses.

Lake Quinault Lodge looks as if it grew naturally on the lake's southern shore. The rustic, two-story lodge has stood since 1926 — long enough for the rain to weather its cedar shakes and the forest to nestle up to it. Even the addition, built in 1989, blends well with the landscape.

The Olympic National Forest cooperates with Lake Quinault Lodge to offer interpretive programs during the busy summer season and several week-long seminars for older people, called Elderhostels, during the winter months.

Lodge guests and campers can walk along the Quinault Rain Forest Nature Trail, either with a Forest Service interpreter or on their own. Signs along this half-mile, flat loop trail tell the story of the rain forest. More energetic hikers can stride the four miles of the Quinault Loop Trail that travel along the lake's shore and deep into the rain forest. Those with a hunger for challenge, solitude, and panoramic views can tackle the fourteen-mile round-trip trail that climbs to the subalpine ridges of the Colonel Bob Wilderness.

The Quinault Lake Loop Auto Tour is a twenty-five mile drive around Quinault Lake with view of the lake, the Quinault River, and thick stands of trees. Some lucky visitors see Roosevelt elk. The tour also passes private resorts and abandoned homesteads and enters Olympic National Park along the Quinault River.

The rhododendron can grow more than twelve feet high, rivaling the size of small trees. This evergreen, which blooms in spectacular clusters of large flowers in May and June, is the state flower of Washington.
PAT O'HARA

101 loop can start at Shelton and drive north along Hood Canal. After a few miles, a side road along the Hamma Hamma River takes visitors to the Hamma Hamma Guard Station. This single-story wooden building with a gabled roof and hexagonal observation room sits on a knoll overlooking the Hamma Hamma Valley.

Participants in the 1930s federal work program, the Civilian Conservation Corps, built the guard station and hundreds of other structures on the Olympic National Forest. The hand-carved shutters and hand-crafted iron hinges of this structure show why CCC projects are known for quality workmanship.

History buffs may also want to visit the Interrorem

Guard Station, picnic area, and self-guided nature trail on the Duckabush River, farther north. The Forest Service built this structure in 1907, just after the agency was created. The Hood Canal District uses the Interrorem Guard Station as a base for fire prevention and for housing seasonal staff. It is one of the oldest national forest buildings still in use in the nation.

Seal Rock Campground, on the Quilcene District a few miles north on Highway 101, is the only salt-water access on a national forest in Washington state. Campers and day-use visitors harvest oysters along the rocky beach of Hood Canal. The campground has water, pit toilets, and campsites with tables and fire grates.

Today's oyster pickers are following in an 800-year-old tradition at Seal Rock. Long before Columbus reached America, Indians at Seal Rock began pitching their summer camps near the beach and fishing for salmon, harpooning seals, hunting deer, digging clams, and picking oysters. They piled empty shells in garbage heaps that remain today. These "shell middens," containing animal bones and discarded tools, are a valuable archaeological record of the lives of prehistoric people.

The Shell Midden Interpretive Trail travels one-quarter mile in a Douglas-fir forest and along the beach in the campground. Illustrated signs tell of ancient and

A saltwater beach in a national forest? These Olympic National Forest beachcombers can take home shellfish to cook over their campfire in the Seal Rock Campground. SCOTT SPIKER

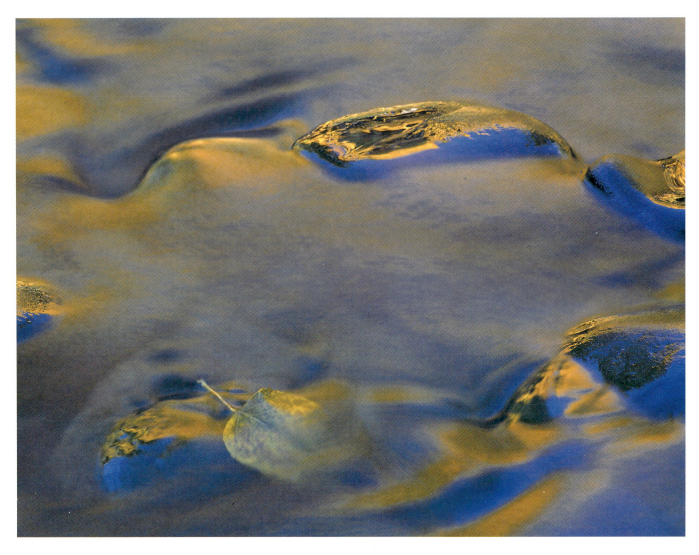

Sunlight creates abstract art as it reflects off the curves and ripples of the Soleduck River, above. PAT O'HARA

The wet, drippy forests of the Olympic Peninsula host a rich collection of fungi, right. Fungi are not parasites, but feed on decaying plants. The fruiting bodies visible at the surface produce spores that can be spread by wind, water, and animals. LEE MANN

modern Indian life and about archaeological findings at the site.

North of Seal Rock, mountain bikers can take a side road to the Lower Quilcene Trail, a six-mile trail in the woods along the Big Quilcene River. Some bikers add twelve miles of road to the trip, making it into a loop with frequent views of the Olympic Mountains.

Side roads off the Hood Canal section of Highway 101 lead to trailheads for the Buckhorn, Brothers, Wonder Mountain, and Mount Skokomish wildernesses. All offer challenging trips into the high country of the eastern Olympic Mountains.

Marmot Pass, in the Buckhorn Wilderness, allows hikers a rare chance to visit a glacial refugium, an area that remained ice-free during the height of the last Ice Age. Three thousand acres of rare plant communities around Marmot Pass have been designated the Buckhorn Mountain Botanical Area, one of twelve botanical areas on the Olympic National Forest.

Some species of plants in the national forest are found only within the Buckhorn Mountain Botanical Area. The closest other examples grow hundreds of miles away, on the eastern side of the Cascade Range. Other species near Marmot Pass developed in the isolation of the Olympic Mountains and are found nowhere else.

The west side of the national forest offers botanical areas as well, such as the Pine Mountain, Old Alaska Yellow Cedar Botanical Area on the Soleduck Ranger District. These 428 acres grow large Alaska yellow cedar that are more than 1,000 years old.

When visitors reach the western side of the Olympic Peninsula they find larger trees, longer rivers, and more rain than on the eastern side. On the Soleduck Ranger District, recreationists can visit a nationally recognized fish enhancement project near Klahowya Campground, a short drive off Highway 101 along the Soleduck River. The Pioneer's Pass Nature Trail in the campground interprets the history of the area.

As visitors drive south, they enter the Lake Quinault Ranger District. A turn off the highway leads to Lake Quinault, a large lowland lake. The Lake Quinault Recreation Area offers an historic lodge, an information center, campgrounds, and trails.

The long, meandering rivers that flow off the western slopes of the Olympic Mountains offer excellent fishing. These anglers with their guide are fishing the Soleduck River for steelhead, a large trout.
PAT O'HARA

The last leg of the Olympic Peninsula loop drive takes travelers east on Highway 101 from Aberdeen to Shelton. Side roads into the national forest provide access to the campgrounds, boat launches, and picnic areas of the Wynoochee Reservoir.

The highway around the Olympic Peninsula can be driven in a day, but the side trips can provide days and weeks of enjoyment. Those who explore the heart of the Olympic National Forest find ecosystems, resource harvests, human cultures, and recreational opportunities woven together into a web of human and natural processes unique to the geographic "island" of the Olympic Peninsula. ■

The Pacific treefrog congregates in open ponds and swamps to breed in the spring. The croaking of the males fills the air at night for several weeks. Most frogs leave the water after mating. The fingers and toes of tree frogs are tipped with little pads that allow them to cling to surfaces as slick as glass. STEVE M. ALDEN

OLYMPIC
NATIONAL FOREST DIRECTORY

POINTS OF INTEREST

SEAL ROCK CAMPGROUND, nestled along the rocky shore of Hood Canal, provides visitors the opportunity to camp in a woodsy setting, harvest shellfish, and learn more about the archaeological significance of the area.

OLYMPIC RAIN FOREST is located on the west side of the Olympic Peninsula and provides a chance to visit one of the few temperate rain forests in the world. Nature trails wind through lush, moist stands of trees that receive more than 200 inches of rainfall each year.

WYNOOCHEE RESERVOIR, measuring 4.4 miles from the concrete dam to where it is fed by the Wynoochee River, provides a pleasant setting for boating, fishing, and swimming. Interpretive exhibits are located at the dam, and camping, picnicking, and hiking opportunities are tucked away in the trees along the shore.

WILDERNESSES

BUCKHORN 44,258 on the east side of the national forest, featuring a wide variety of vegetation.

THE BROTHERS 16,412 acres of steep, forested slopes on the east side of the national forest.

MOUNT SKOKOMISH 13,015 acres of steep, rugged terrain on the southeast side of the national forest.

COLONEL BOB 11,961 acres on the west side of the national forest, near Lake Quinault.

WONDER MOUNTAIN 2,349 acres provide a scenic backdrop for Lake Cushman, on the south side of the national forest.

RECREATIONAL OPPORTUNITIES

HIKING AND RIDING More than 200 miles of trails provide access to wilderness areas, rustic camping areas, scenic viewpoints, lakes, and streams. Several trails, including the Quinault Rain Forest and Interrorem nature trails, are popular roadside walks. Many trails connect with the Olympic National Park trail system.

CAMPING Twenty campgrounds with approximately 450 sites, ranging from developed sites to more primitive settings.

SCENIC DRIVES U.S. Highway 101 makes a 340-mile scenic loop around the national forest, providing a chance to visit a number of natural, historical, and cultural sites. Motorists may choose from more than 2,500 miles of maintained roads to explore valleys and ridges of the national forest.

BOATING, SWIMMING, AND SCUBA DIVING The Olympic Peninsula is bordered on three sides by salt water and speckled with numerous freshwater lakes — such as Lake Quinault, Lake Cushman and Wynoochee Reservoir — that offer many opportunities to enjoy the water.

BEACHCOMBING AND GATHERING SHELLFISH The 2,700 feet of saltwater shoreline and tidelands at Seal Rock Campground offer visitors the chance to collect clams, oysters, crabs, and other beach treasures.

HUNTING Elk, deer, bear, and grouse. Regulated by Washington Department of Wildlife.

FISHING Trout, salmon, and steelhead in season. Regulated by the Washington Department of Fisheries and the Indian tribes.

OFF-ROAD VEHICLES The Olympic Peninsula offers several off-road vehicle opportunities. More information on regulations and locations is available at ranger stations.

MOUNTAIN BIKES Although not specifically designed for mountain bike use, thirty trails totaling eighty-five miles are open to bikes on the national forest.

ADMINISTRATIVE OFFICES

FOREST HEADQUARTERS 1835 Blacklake Blvd., Olympia, WA 98502 (206) 956-2300

HOOD CANAL RANGER STATION P.O. Box 68, Hoodsport, WA 98548 (206) 877-5254

QUILCENE RANGER STATION P.O. Box 280, Quilcene, WA 98376 (206) 765-3368

QUINAULT RANGER STATION Route 1, Box 9, Quinault, WA 98575 (206) 288-2525

SOLEDUCK RANGER STATION R.R. 1, Box 5750, Forks, WA 98331 (206) 374-6522

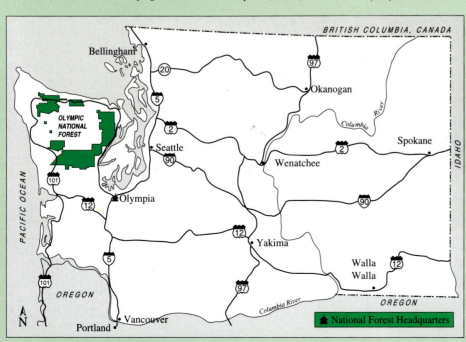

Autumn oranges and reds of huckleberry, heather, and mountain ash contrast with the glacial white of 10,778-foot Mount Baker, the northernmost volcano in Washington state. LEE MANN

Mount Baker-Snoqualmie

N A T I O N A L   F O R E S T

Escape from the city

Rush hour in Seattle — cars are crawling along the freeway. Horns honk, and fumes pour from exhaust pipes. Drivers hunch over their steering wheels, necks tensed, heads pounding, and stomachs tied in knots. Is there relief from the stress of urban life? Yes. It's called the Mount Baker-Snoqualmie National Forest.

A Seattle resident can reach the national forest boundary within an hour. Beyond that brown, wooden entrance sign, corridors of trees replace canyons of high-rises, brisk mountain breezes clear the air, and the sounds of rushing water soothe ears bruised by urban noise.

The Mount Baker-Snoqualmie National Forest blankets the west slopes of the Cascade Range for 130 miles between the Canadian border and Mount Rainier National Park.

Almost three million people live near the national forest in western Washington. Another four million live within a two-hour drive, in Vancouver, British Columbia, the third-largest city in Canada. The Mount Baker-Snoqualmie National Forest records more than fifteen million visitor days each year, making it one of the most visited national forests in the nation.

What do all these urban escapees find when they get to the national forest? Wildernesses offer solitude and magnificent views. Lakes provide opportunities for

The Glacier Public Service Center is the gateway to the Mount Baker Scenic Byway. The Civilian Conservation Corps built the center in 1937 and 1938, in what is known as the Cascadian style of architecture. The center now contains interpretive exhibits on the building itself, as well as features in the area.
JIM McDONALD

Outdoor kiosks at the Glacier Public Service Center offer twenty-four hour information about recreational opportunities in the North Fork Nooksack Valley. JIM BELANGER

fishing, boating, and swimming. Rivers and streams beckon rafters, while mountains challenge climbers. Campgrounds offer rest for travelers.

Six major rivers in the national forest flow west from the crest of the Cascades to the Puget Sound lowlands. Each drainage — with its steep-sided valleys carved by glaciers — is a self-contained recreation package with trails, campgrounds, picnic areas, information stations, and unique recreational highlights.

The North Fork of the Nooksack River, farthest north, is paralleled by the Mount Baker Scenic Byway, a paved, winding road that travels past historic buildings, through thick woods, and up to the Heather Meadows recreation area, where glaciers cover some of the tallest peaks in the range.

Along the byway, anglers can cast lines into trout-filled streams, hikers can stretch their legs on invigorating day hikes, and photographers can snap pictures of jagged mountaintops. Stops include the scenic Nooksack Falls, where the north fork of the river thunders over a 175-foot cliff, and the interpretive exhibits at the Glacier Public Service Center.

A nine-mile side trip up the Glacier Creek Road takes sightseers to the Mount Baker Vista. Here Mount Baker, a volcano, rises like a huge, ice-covered octopus. The Heliotrope Ridge Trail in the Mount Baker Wilderness takes adventurous climbers to the edge of a great ice tentacle.

The Skagit River, the next valley south, is famous

for its bald eagles. This federally designated Wild and Scenic River flows cold and clear and is filled with spawning salmon during late summer, autumn, and early winter. Bald eagles flock to the river from October to March, to feast on the fish. As many as 600 eagles perch in the cottonwoods along the river each year.

A paved side road off Washington Highway 20 heads north to Baker Lake, a ten-mile dammed reservoir with dramatic views of 10,788-foot Mount Baker and 9,127-foot Mount Shuksan. Boat launches in the campgrounds allow anglers to try their luck almost every day of the fishing season.

The Shadow of the Sentinels interpretive trail, accessible to handicapped people, starts at a parking area on the main road and winds through some of the largest Douglas-fir still standing in the Pacific Northwest. Other trails for hikers and horses ascend into the Mount Baker and Noisy-Diobsud wildernesses. Backcountry routes into the Mount Baker National Recreation Area are open to snowmobiles in the winter.

Continuing south, the two forks of the Stillaguamish River create a pair of valleys. The Mountain Loop Scenic Byway allows visitors to go up one fork of the river and come

---

The glaciers on Mount Baker provide varying degrees of difficulty for mountaineers. Experienced climbers tackle routes with sheer ice walls and yawning crevasses. Beginners ascend the Coleman Glacier, above left, the easy way to the summit. WILLIAM L. BATES

Hundreds of bald eagles migrate south to the Skagit River from Alaska and Canada during the winter. The eagles feed on dead salmon that wash up on gravel bars. The salmon die naturally after spawning. TOM AND PAT LEESON

down the other. Near the town of Darrington, the North Fork Stillaguamish Valley opens wide for views of the rocky, glacier-laden summits of Whitehorse and Three Fingers mountains and the thick woods of the Boulder River Wilderness.

The byway turns south at Darrington and follows the Sauk River, a designated Wild and Scenic River, upstream for a few miles. Drivers often stop to gaze into pools of deep blue water between tumbling rapids. Side roads along this section of the highway lead to trailheads for the spectacular high country of the Glacier Peak and Henry M. Jackson wildernesses.

At Barlow Pass — the divide between the Sauk and South Fork of the Stillaguamish rivers — a five-mile stroll up a side road takes people to the historic mining town of Monte Cristo. Here, at the turn of the century, thousands of miners sought, but failed, to find their fortune. The town now consists of a few rotting timbers poking through the underbrush.

Down the South Fork, the road travels past the ruins of the historic Big Four Lodge. Those who stop here can hike an easy boardwalk trail to ice caves at the base of the vertical wall of Big Four Mountain.

The byway also takes in the Verlot Public Service Center, built by the Civilian Conservation Corps in the 1930s. This historic building contains visitor information and interpretive displays.

The Skykomish Valley is next. U.S. Highway 2 enters the forest from the west along the Skykomish River. The yawning, U-shaped valley seems to swal-

Mount Shuksan casts its reflection into Picture Lake at Heather Meadows, on ridges above the Nooksack River Valley. Mount Shuksan, 9,127 feet in height, is one of the tallest non-volcanic peaks in the Cascades.
CHARLES GURCHE

LANDS THAT RESIST AND THREATEN

It's easy to get lost in the Upper Suiattle River Valley. The trail fades away after a few miles. The roar of the river blends with the roars of its tributaries. The old trees are tall, and the valley bottom is flat, making it difficult to see far.

Wandering alone and disoriented in a trailess forest twenty miles from the nearest road can be frightening. The dangers are real. Streams raging with glacier melt must be crossed without bridges. Rain, and even snow, can fall almost any day of the year, making travel dangerous for the unprepared hiker. Bear and cougar still roam these woods. The trails are often steep and hard to follow. Few signs guide the way.

The Upper Suiattle is one of the many risk-filled corners of the Glacier Peak Wilderness. Other wildernesses in the Mount Baker-Snoqualmie National Forest have their share of steep cliffs, glacial crevasses, and poisonous plants that pose dangers for backcountry users who don't take the proper precautions or pack the right equipment.

These lands remain wild by order of Congress. Those who want to stay safe at any cost should never step foot into the wilderness — an area that is supposed to challenge, test survival skills, and provide glimpses of what vast stretches of wild land our continent used to be. When entering one of the eight wildernesses on the national forest, be prepared for risk and challenge.

Keeping wildernesses wild requires some rules and regulations. The Mount Baker-Snoqualmie National Forest applies as few as possible, respecting the freedom and spontaneity that make the wilderness experience so precious.

Permits limit the numbers of visitors in some areas, and party size in all wilderness areas is limited to twelve. Most areas above timberline are closed to campfires, and all trash must be packed out. The rules are summarized by the familiar Forest Service slogan, "Walk softly, take only photographs, and leave only footprints."

A few days in the Upper Suiattle can provide treasures found few other places: a flowered seat high on the side of a mountain with glaciers looming above, mountain goats clambering up nearby ridges, and a river roaring far below in the valley — an untouched crop of fat blue huckleberries — bright flags of yellow monkey flowers tufting from gravel bars between luminous streams of river.

But Henry David Thoreau may have captured the rarest and most important gift wilderness offers: "It would be worthwhile to tell why a swamp pleases us. . . . Why the moaning of the storm gives me pleasure. . . our spirits revive like lichens in the storm. There is something worth living when we are resisted, threatened. I sometimes feel that I need to sit in a faraway cave through a three weeks' storm, cold and wet to give tone to my system."

If Thoreau still lived, he might take heart that we have preserved lands that resist and threaten us. And he could find his cave and his storm and the solitude to experience them in the wildernesses of the Mount Baker-Snoqualmie National Forest.

Hiking trails in the Mount Baker Wilderness offer spectacular views of Mount Shuksan. SCOTT SPIKER

Mount Index rises to 5,979 feet above sea level, standing like a sentry at the entrance to the Skykomish River Valley. DAVID SCOTT

low the highway, which takes travelers to a sudden view of the rocky spire of Mount Index.

Highway 2 leads up to Stevens Pass, one of the lower passes in the Cascade Range. James J. Hill chose this route in the 1890s for the Great Northern Railway. Today, a relocated, modern railway parallels the historic rail route over Stevens Pass.

The Great Northern Railway route is part of the Stevens Pass Historic District. Visitors who explore the abandoned railway grade find collapsed tunnels and snowsheds. Signs tell the story of tunnels dug with hand tools, trains destroyed by avalanches, and the indomitable spirit of early railroaders.

In 1889, the last spike was driven in the tracks near Deception Falls, a few miles below Stevens Pass. Interpretive signs in the picnic area near the falls commemorate the occasion.

Deception Falls plummets sixty feet along the highway. A mile-long interpretive trail skirts the rocky gorge of the

Alpental Ski Area is one of four ski areas at Snoqualmie Pass, only an hour east of Seattle on Interstate 90. Many urban dwellers change from office clothes to ski parkas and drive to Snoqualmie Pass for night skiing after work. BOB AND IRA SPRING

Tye River, where whitewater and shaggy old trees make highways and cities seem a distant memory.

Other recreational opportunities in the Skykomish Valley include rock climbing near Mount Index and rafting over Boulder Drop, a challenging rapid in the Skykomish River. Winter visitors cross-country ski or ride snowmobiles over miles of snow-covered national forests roads.

Farther south, beyond the peaks and waters of the Alpine Lakes Wilderness, the Snoqualmie River flows alongside Interstate 90, the major route between Seattle and Boston. The Snoqualmie Valley is proof that you don't have to be going to the national forest to get there. Millions of travelers pass through this valley on their way to other destinations.

Campgrounds along the four-lane highway are noted with large, lighted signs over the freeway, rather than the small wooden signs that are more typical of national forest sites. The rustic camping conditions here contrast with the ultra-modern highway.

Hikers in this area can stop at the Granite Mountain trailhead for an exhilarating hike to Granite Peak fire lookout. This old firewatch tower looks out over the peaks and lake basins of the Alpine Lakes Wilderness. Glaciers sculpted the rugged topography from the hard granite that makes up the core of the Cascade Range.

Even travelers on a fast track might want to stop at Snoqualmie Pass. A short drive off the highway takes visitors to Gold Creek Pond, a reclaimed gravel pit that has become a haven for elk, beaver, Canadian geese, and fish. Forest Service biologists have installed nesting boxes and improved fishways. A picnic area and an interpretive trail are located at the edge of the pond.

The White River Valley lies the farthest south in the national forest. The White River flows around the north side of 14,410-foot Mount Rainier. This valley

A vantage point near Stevens Pass at the crest of the Cascade Range offers a spectacular view of the Skykomish River Valley and the setting sun. SCOTT PRICE

Mountain goats are native to the Cascade Range. These members of the antelope family climb with agility, thanks to the "suction-cup" action of their hooves. The nannies and kids travel in herds, led by the dominant female. The billies usually live alone, joining the herd only during the fall breeding season.
TOM AND PAT LEESON

Mount Baker is an active volcano. Steam still pours from cracks in the glaciers in Sherman Crater, near the volcano's summit. In 1974 and 1975, steam increased and a lake formed in the crater. Since then, steam activity has decreased, and the lake has refrozen. LEE MANN

contains the Mather Memorial Parkway, which travels up through the Mount Baker-Snoqualmie National Forest into Mount Rainier National Park and then east to the Wenatchee National Forest.

Elk herds graze year-round in the open areas and woods along the parkway. Mountain goats forage on volcanic cliffs along the river. Those who take side trips up to higher ground, such as the summit of Suntop Mountain, can see such wildlife as grouse, marmots, and pikas. A rehabilitated fire lookout perches atop Suntop, and visitors are welcome to drive up and share the 360-degree view with the volunteer on duty.

History buffs and four-wheel-drive enthusiasts may want to take the side trip to the Naches Wagon Road. Pioneers lowered their wagons with ropes over the cliffs on this trail. Four-wheelers have been known to do the same.

The streamside campsites in the Dalles Campground provide peaceful overnight stays. Visitors may also want to stop at the campground and walk the Dalles Trail, which winds among 300-year-old grand fir rooted in the remains of one of the largest volcanic mudflows in the world.

In the winter, most of the cars on the road are headed for Crystal Mountain Ski Area, one of seven commercial ski areas on the national forest. Like its counter-

A hiker pausing among a stand of old-growth trees in the Glacier Peak Wilderness can appreciate the size such mature trees can reach. LEE MANN

LANDSCAPE BY GEOLOGICAL CONSENT

Tomyhoi Peak, 6,145 feet tall, rises from ridges near the Canadian border. Hikers ascend a trail to Yellow Aster Meadows, where they can enjoy wildflowers, small lakes, and climbs to the rocky summit. LARRY·ULRICH

There are few views on earth as magnificent as those at Heather Meadows. In one direction, the glacier-hung crags of Mount Shuksan stab the sky. In another, the huge, ice-shrouded dome of Mount Baker swells up from a sea of smaller peaks. The word "breathtaking" takes on a literal meaning at this Forest Service recreation area at the end of the Mount Baker Scenic Byway.

And it's not just the peaks. Heather and huckleberry meadows roll for miles. Glistening lakes nestle between knolls. Ridges bristle with 900-year-old mountain hemlock trees. Mountain goats graze among the crags, and migratory birds ride the wind over the passes.

Even the rocks catch the eye. Eruptions from Mount Baker have spewed layer after layer of lava during the last 500,000 years. Lava flows resisted glacial carving and stand up like black anvils against the sky. Lava cooled and cracked into six-sided columns, creating cliff faces that look like artistically arranged organ pipes.

The Ice Age hasn't been gone long at Heather Meadows. This undulating lava plateau remained ice-covered for thousands of years after glaciers retreated from most of the Cascade Range. Today, smaller alpine glaciers still carve the sides of the tallest mountains — reminders that the ocean of ice may have only temporarily ebbed from this place.

An ice age is easy to imagine at Heather Meadows in January. Most winters, more than twenty feet of snow stands on the ground, leveling the humps and bumps of the land. Only the upper parts of trees poke up through the snow blanket, often encased in ice. Most animals hibernate, and streams freeze. When the ski area is closed, it seems as if all life has fled from the cold and snow.

The summer is another matter. When heather is blooming, insects are buzzing, and swallows are skimming over lakes rippling in the sun, ice seems only a pessimist's nightmare. It takes the eye of a geologist to recognize that the smooth rocks and the lake basins

Picture Lake nestles among meadows and mountain hemlock trees at Heather Meadows, a recreation area at the eastern end of the Mount Baker Scenic Byway. The Canadian border runs through the peaks in the distance. PENNY FALKNOR

were recently gouged by glaciers.

Plants condense all their growing and reproduction into the two or three snow-free months here each year. A perceptive biologist, standing among the flowers one August afternoon, commented: "If photosynthesis could be heard, a symphony would be playing."

Hoary marmots, like other permanent meadow residents, eat with forethought all summer. By October they can barely waddle to their winter burrows. Migratory species such as mountain goats follow the melting snow upward during the summer until they graze where the highest plants meet rock and ice. When they head downslope in the fall, snow is just around the corner.

Mountain goats aren't the only species to use Heather Meadows seasonally. People, too, migrate in and out depending on their interests. Heather Meadows is a commercial ski area in the winter and a national forest day-use recreation area year-round.

This area used to be a secret. In the 1920s, visitors came from around the country to stay in a short-lived luxury lodge. Between then and the 1980s, mostly locals from Bellingham and a few people from Canada traveled the winding mountain road to Heather Meadows.

But, largely by word of mouth, the area has been discovered. It's common to find hundreds of cars in the parking lots, hikers lining the trails, sightseers crowding the viewpoints, or skiers thick on the slopes. Automobile advertisements have been filmed in front of the mountain backdrops, and Heather Meadows vistas appear on calendars and even wallpaper.

As an increasing number of people visit Heather Meadows, the Forest Service has upgraded roads, restrooms, and hiking trails. Interpretive signs and ranger-guided walks now allow visitors a glimpse into the stories behind the scenery.

The Forest Service also is trying to prevent damage to the fragile meadow ecosystem. Overused side trails have been closed and revegetated. A viewing platform at the tender shores of a lake gives people a place to stand, while protecting plants and animals from trampling. Educational signs and programs encourage respect for the organisms that make Heather Meadows their home.

The glaciers and volcanic eruptions that shaped Heather Meadows in the past could change the landscape again in the future. This area's beauty is made more poignant by the knowledge that it exists, as philosopher-historian Will Durant once said, "by geological consent, subject to change without notice."

New growth covers the ground, above, where timber has been harvested. When most of the trees are removed from an area during one harvest, the resulting bald patch is called a clearcut. Some tree species, such as Douglas-fir, must be planted in open areas like these in order to regenerate. SONNY PAZ

Wild ducks get a helping hand from Forest Service biologists, left, who install nesting boxes on trees near lakes and streams. SONNY PAZ

The spiky blossoms of the long-growing Indian paintbrush stand above other meadow wildflowers. TOM AND PAT LEESON

parts at Mount Baker, Stevens Pass, and Snoqualmie Pass, Crystal Mountain operates on national forest land under a special-use permit.

Crystal Mountain hosts a hefty share of the one million people who ski the national forest slopes each year. From the top of the lifts, skiers see a panorama of the southern Cascades, including views of Mount Rainier drenched in winter snow.

Urban dwellers from Tacoma to Vancouver, British Columbia, cherish the Mount Baker-Snoqualmie

Western redcedar trees thrive in the wet, cool climate of the west slopes of the Cascades. Cedar bark and wood were used by early Indians for longhouses, clothing, canoes, and baskets.
LEE MANN

National Forest for its recreational opportunities. But this is no national park. More than 200 million board feet of timber was harvested annually on the national forest in recent years. Woodcutters take home truckloads of firewood. Hundreds of thousands of tons of gravel are mined for highway construction. Water is dammed for hydroelectric power channeled to cities on the west side of the Cascades. Consumptive recreational uses such as fishing and hunting are allowed.

Mount Baker-Snoqualmie managers share the same directive as their counterparts on other national forests: to balance the many different uses of the national forest in a way that benefits the greatest number of people while maintaining the long-term health of the ecosystem. Controversy often occurs over which uses will take precedence.

Thus public involvement is vital in deciding the fate of an ecosystem, a rare species, a recreational opportunity, or a proposed development. And the people in the Puget Sound area care about the national forest. Thousands of citizens each year provide vigorous and informed input to Forest Service decisions.

The Mount Baker-Snoqualmie National Forest is front-page news in Puget Sound communities, and the

Northern spotted owls are one of several wildlife species that depend on mature forests for survival. The spotted owl is listed as a threatened species by the U.S. Fish and Wildlife Service.
TOM AND PAT LEESON

issues that stir debate are often complex.

The issue of harvesting old-growth timber, which is home to the spotted owl, is just one example. That issue has sparked vociferous public debate at not only the regional level, but also the national level.

While walking among the wildflowers on a wilderness ridgetop, skiing through newly fallen snow, or stalking a deer in the autumn woods, it's hard to remember that the Mount Baker-Snoqualmie National Forest generates such controversy.

Each recreational experience, each timber harvest, each intact ecosystem here is no accident. They are all part of a complicated resource balancing act by Forest Service professionals.

Add good will, up-to-date research, and public involvement to the land management equation, and the Mount Baker-Snoqualmie National Forest will continue to thrive and meet the needs of the millions of people living at its edges. ■

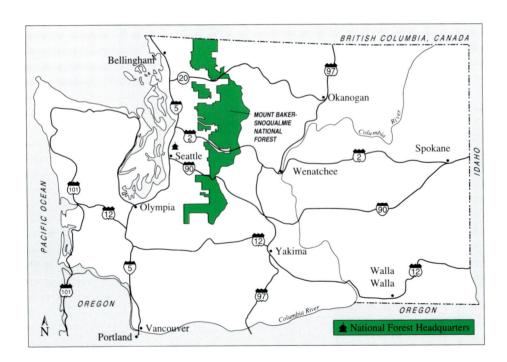

MOUNT BAKER-SNOQUALMIE
NATIONAL FOREST DIRECTORY

POINTS OF INTEREST

HEATHER MEADOWS RECREATION AREA in subalpine meadows between Mount Baker and Mount Shuksan at the end of the Mount Baker Scenic Byway. The area offers spectacular views, numerous recreational opportunities, and access to the Mount Baker Wilderness.

MOUNT BAKER NATIONAL RECREATION AREA 8,600 acres on the southern slopes of Mount Baker provide snowmobiling in the winter and hiking and horseback riding in the summer.

SKAGIT WILD AND SCENIC RIVER 158 miles of rivers with outstanding scenery, recreation, and wildlife. Includes portions of the Skagit, Cascade, Suiattle, and Sauk rivers. Noted for winter bald eagle viewing.

WILDERNESSES

MOUNT BAKER 122,676 acres around the glaciated volcano of Mount Baker, with hiking trails in forests and meadows.

NOISY-DIOBSUD 15,015 acres east of Baker Lake in remote, subalpine terrain near Mount Watson.

BOULDER RIVER 50,388 acres of a valley forested with old-growth timber at the base of Three Fingers Mountain.

GLACIER PEAK 282,267 acres on the national forest, on the western side of Glacier Peak east of Darrington.

HENRY M. JACKSON 75,836 acres on the national forest, at the crest of the Cascades north of Stevens Pass.

ALPINE LAKES 145,348 acres on the national forest, containing rugged peaks and mountain lakes between Stevens Pass and Snoqualmie Pass.

CLEARWATER 14,255 isolated acres north of Mount Rainier and Mount Rainier National Park.

NORSE PEAK 15,923 acres of peaks and ridges east of Mount Rainier near Highway 410. Additional acres on the Wenatchee National Forest.

RECREATIONAL OPPORTUNITIES

HIKING AND RIDING 1,430 miles of trails, including ninety-six miles of the Pacific Crest National Scenic Trail in the Cascade Range. Short hikes to scenic views and sites include the half-mile, barrier-free Shadow of the Sentinels Trail near Baker Lake, the one-mile Ice Caves Trail near Verlot, and the one-mile Deception Falls Natural Trail on the Skykomish Ranger District.

CAMPING AND PICNICKING Thirty-nine developed campgrounds with 1,596 campsites. Fees charged at some full-service campgrounds.

SCENIC DRIVES Mount Baker Scenic Byway, a winding, paved road into the northernmost valley of the national forest, includes twenty-four miles of Washington Highway 542 east of Bellingham. The Mountain Loop Scenic Byway passes through thick woods and past fast-running rivers, between Granite Falls and Darrington.

KAYAKING AND CANOEING Many rivers on the national forest offer challenging whitewater from June through September.

HUNTING Deer, elk, black bear, and grouse throughout the national forest. Washington state licenses and game regulations apply.

FISHING Cutthroat, rainbow, and other species of trout, steelhead, and salmon throughout the national forest.

ALPINE SKIING Mount Baker Ski Area (six chairlifts), fifty miles east of Bellingham on Washington Highway 542; Stevens Pass Ski Area (eight chairlifts), fifty miles east of Everett on Washington Highway 2; Snoqualmie Pass (eight chairlifts), Alpental (four chairlifts), Ski Acres (seven chairlifts), and Pac West (three chairlifts) ski areas, all approximately fifty miles east of Seattle on Interstate 90; and Crystal Mountain Ski Area (nine chairlifts), fifty miles east of Tacoma on Washington Highway 410.

CROSS-COUNTRY SKIING 129 miles of groomed trails plus thousands of miles of forest roads.

SNOWMOBILING 200 miles of groomed forest roads and trails plus thousands of miles of forest roads.

OFF-ROAD VEHICLES Twenty-six miles of trail. Drivers must be licensed; vehicles must be street legal and licensed or have ORV permit.

ADMINISTRATIVE OFFICES

FOREST HEADQUARTERS 21905 64th Ave., Mountlake Terrace, WA 98043 (206) 775-9702

MOUNT BAKER RANGER STATION 2105 Highway 20, Sedro Woolley, WA 98284 (206) 856-5700; Glacier Public Service Center, Glacier, WA 98244 (206) 599-2714

DARRINGTON RANGER STATION 1405 Emmons St., Darrington, WA 98241 (206) 436-1155; Verlot Public Service Center, Verlot, WA 98252 (206) 691-7791

SKYKOMISH RANGER STATION 74920 N.E. Stevens Pass Highway, P.O. Box 305, Skykomish, WA 98288 (206) 677-2414

NORTH BEND RANGER STATION 42404 S.E. North Bend Way, North Bend, WA 98045 (206) 888-1421; Snoqualmie Pass Visitor Center (206) 434-6111

WHITE RIVER RANGER STATION 853 Roosevelt Ave. E., Enumclaw, WA 98022 (206) 825-6585

OUTDOOR RECREATION INFORMATION CENTER 915 Second Ave., Room 442, Seattle, WA 98174 (206) 553-0170

Morning sun reflects in still waters at Boulder Pass in the Glacier Peak Wilderness. Boulder Pass is on the divide between the White River Valley and the Napeequa River Valley, on the Wenatchee National Forest. PAT O'HARA

Wenatchee
N A T I O N A L F O R E S T

From glaciers to sagebrush

Water flows east in the Wenatchee National Forest, descending from the 8,000-foot crest of the Cascade Range to the Columbia River at 700 feet above sea level. Streams melted from glaciers meander through subalpine meadows, tumble over waterfalls, race down timbered hillsides, and flow through sagebrush-covered hills.

The Wenatchee National Forest in central Washington shares the eastern slopes of the Cascades with the Okanogan National Forest to the north and the Yakima Indian Reservation to the south. Covering 2.2 million acres, the Wenatchee is the largest national forest in Washington.

The national forest frequently basks in sunny, dry weather created by the rainshadow of the Cascade Range. Wet clouds blowing in from the Pacific rise over the Cascades and drop most of their moisture on the mountains' western slopes. Clouds east of the crest often are puffy white cumulus, wrung dry and rainless.

Distribution of precipitation over the thirty-mile width of the national forest creates striking differences between ecosystems. A meadow at the crest receives 120 inches of moisture a year. The pine forests below receive just thirty inches. By the time the clouds float out over the rolling hills near the Columbia River, they drop only ten inches of precipitation a year, barely enough to support sagebrush and jackrabbits.

A flight over the 135-mile length of the national

The rugged slopes of 8,182-foot Gilbert Peak are typical of the raw beauty of mountains within the Goat Rocks Wilderness, south of White Pass on the Naches Ranger District. The peak looms above the North Fork Tieton River drainage. RICK STOCKWELL

forest verifies its diversity. Start at the north, at the Okanogan National Forest boundary. Fly along 55-mile Lake Chelan, the third-deepest lake in North America. Pass ice-shrouded Glacier Peak to the west, a 10,500-foot sleeping volcano surrounded by rugged wilderness.

Below, silver rivers flash by, carrying glacial melt from the peaks to the Columbia. First Entiat, then Chiwawa, Wenatchee, Teanaway, Yakima, Naches, and Tieton. The Indian names translate to such watery phrases as "river flowing from canyon," and "plenty of water."

Cross U.S. Highway 2 and Interstate 90, the Amtrak railroad line, and an historic railway. Look west into the Alpine Lakes Wilderness between Stevens and Snoqualmie passes. Glaciers flash white, hanging from dark crags. Small, round lakes glisten blue on mountain shoulders. Green forest aprons spread down ridges. Streams flow in valley bottoms like silver ribbons.

Look east. A few white cotton clouds float in a bright blue sky. Forests thin until pine gives way to sagebrush. At the eastern edge of the national forest, the mighty Columbia River hugs dry, brown foothills. Beyond the river stretches the flat lava plateau of eastern Washington.

Fly farther south over the Norse Peak and William O. Douglas wildernesses. To the west, Mount Rainier — the largest and tallest volcano in the Cascades — soars to 14,410 feet.

The flight ends at the Wenatchee National Forest's

southern boundary after crossing Rimrock Lake, a Forest Service recreation area and an irrigation reservoir for the Yakima Valley. Farther south lies the Yakima Indian Reservation.

Your trip covered hundreds of ecosystems with habitats different enough to host mountain goats and rattlesnakes, elk and otter, salmon and spotted owls. The Wenatchee contains, as well, a wealth of recreational facilities and opportunities — 2,600 miles of trail, 5,000 miles of forest roads, 151 campgrounds, nine proposed Wild and Scenic rivers, seven wildernesses, and seven commercial ski areas.

During the flight, you could have parachuted down into a sparkling mountain lake, a grazing cattle herd, a volcanic crater, an abandoned copper mine, an active logging show, a winding forest trail, a guided nature walk, or a whitewater river.

The Wenatchee records more than ten million visits each year, making it one of the most visited national forests in the nation.

The showy yellow blossoms of balsamroot sprout among boulders at Echo Point near Vantage. The Columbia River flows by in the background.
PAT O'HARA

The Wenatchee also holds an impressive array of resources. Each year, timber harvest provides enough lumber to build 10,000 homes. More than 10,000 cords of firewood from the national forest burn in woodstoves from Yakima to Chelan. Tens of thousands of sheep and cattle graze on national forest range.

Miners remove tens of thousands of tons of gravel deposited by glaciers. Other forest products include cabin logs, fence posts, gold, fish, wild game, huckleberries, and mushrooms.

Each valley, lake, river, road, and mountain on the national forest invites exploration. Look at the map and Lake Chelan stands out as a good place to start — a long blue fjord running fifty-five miles northwest to southeast near the northern tip of the forest. A few miles of the northern end of the lake lie within the Lake Chelan National Recreation Area managed by North Cascades National Park, while the rest is part of the Wenatchee National Forest.

Ice Age glaciers dug and dammed the basin that holds Lake Chelan. The lake level was raised twenty feet when a dam was built in the 1920s to generate

Hikers in the Lake Chelan-Sawtooth Wilderness can choose steep mountain scrambles, meadowed ridge walks, or relatively flat travel along the shores of fifty-five mile Lake Chelan. The clean, clear waters of Lake Chelan contain a variety of fish, from rainbow trout to salmon. PAT O'HARA

Helicopter logging is one way to harvest timber with minimum impact on forest ecosystems. Damage is reduced because the logs are lifted straight up, rather than dragged across the ground. Few roads are necessary, a factor that reduces post-harvest erosion. TOM AND PAT LEESON

From death comes life. This vibrant Pacific red elderberry is fed from the decay of the fallen tree.
RICHARD MURRAY

electricity. Even without that added depth, Lake Chelan still measures 1,486 feet deep. Crater Lake and Lake Tahoe are the only deeper lakes in the United States. If the water was drained out of Lake Chelan and spread over Washington, the state would be under 4.5 inches of water. The gorge left behind would be deeper than the Grand Canyon.

No roads reach the upper two-thirds of Lake Chelan. The Lady of the Lake passenger ferry, private boats, or float planes deliver visitors to the many rustic campsites tucked away in coves along the steep, rocky lake shore. From these jumping-off points, visitors can walk along the lake or venture up trails in side canyons to alpine areas above.

No boat is needed to enjoy the water in the Entiat Valley south of Lake Chelan. A narrow paved road turns off the main highway between Chelan and Wenatchee and follows the gentle curves of the Entiat River upstream for miles.

In the fall, the drive is a visual delight. The river runs clear, cottonwood and aspen trees glow yellow along the river banks, and sumac and Douglas maples color the hillsides with oranges and reds.

Small Forest Service campgrounds abound along the Entiat River. Each has its charms. But Silver Falls Campground wins the blue ribbon for big trees. Large

THE LEGACY OF THE HOLDEN MINE

No roads connect the village of Holden with the outside world. It takes a half-day boat ride up Lake Chelan and a half-hour bus trip up a dead-end road to reach this historic mining site perched near timberline in the Railroad Creek Valley of the Wenatchee National Forest.

The Glacier Peak Wilderness begins a mile from Holden. There are no phones. All vehicles, groceries, and other supplies come by barge up the lake. A church retreat center operates in the old mining townsite buildings. Visitors come to this mountain Shangri-La for refuge from the faster-paced life "down-lake."

Holden's isolation seems precious today, but it wasn't always seen in a positive light. Howe Sound Mining Company found it a major challenge to operate a copper mine profitably at Holden from 1938 to 1957.

Ore had to be trucked to Lake Chelan, shipped by barge to the town of Chelan, and then taken by train across the Cascade Range to Tacoma for smelting. The ore was rich enough with copper, gold, and silver to offset transportation costs. At one time, the Holden Mine was the largest and most technologically advanced mining operation in the state of Washington.

At the site of the historic town that housed workers for the Holden Mine from 1938 to 1957, Holden Village today is a Lutheran retreat center. PAUL HART, JR.

The church retreat buildings at Holden were once a company town for the mine. Houses, a store, school, recreation hall, hospital, soda shop, and bowling alley helped create a community so self-sufficient that it even minted its own money. But the mine closed in 1957, when the ore became depleted and copper prices fell. The townsite was then donated to the Lutheran Church.

The state-of-the-art mill at Holden reduced the 2,000 tons of ore mined daily to 200 tons of higher-grade concentrate. The eight million tons of waste products were piled into mountains of tailings along the banks of Railroad Creek below the mine.

Given the technology of the day, Howe Sound Mining Company attemped to reduce the environmental damage caused by the tailings, building a retaining wall to hold the piles up out of the creek.

For thirty years after the mine's closure, the tailings were a visible reminder of the mining era. Originally gray, they weathered to a bright yellow-orange. Water percolating through these orange mountains polluted Railroad Creek downstream.

The timber wall holding the piles up out of the creek began to rot.

Lakes formed on the flat tops of the piles each spring. On dry summer days, clouds of orange dust rose with the wind. Few plants could grow in this hostile environment. Residents at the nearby retreat center complained about respiratory problems and stream pollution.

The mine and tailings reverted to the Forest Service when the mine closed. In 1989, the agency began a reclamation project to reduce the environmental impact of the mine tailings and speed the natural processes of revegetation at the site. The Holden Mine Reclamation Project reshaped the piles, provided drainage channels to direct runoff away from the tailings, and built a rock wall along the banks of Railroad Creek to prevent floods from washing the tailings downstream.

The project also covered the surface of the piles with gravel, changing the color from orange to a less-visible gray. Eight acres of topsoil islands added on top of the gravel now grow native plants that should spread to cover the piles, blending them with the natural surroundings.

Fisheries enhancement, coordinated with the reclamation project, will improve fish habitat in Railroad Creek by establishing pools, resting areas, and side channels and by breaking up the cemented stream bottom gravels.

The best long-term solution to improving the environmental quality of the Holden Mine site would be to remove the tailings altogether. Someday ore prices may rise and a mining company will be able to profitably remove the tailings for reprocessing. Until then, the piles are stabilized, and their effects on the surrounding environment has been significantly reduced.

Thanks to the reclamation project, the legacy of the Holden Mine is now more one of colorful history than one of pollution. Visitors to Holden today can read interpretive signs at the townsite and the ruined mine and mill structures or browse through the community museum to learn the story of the mining era. Echos of the past, the vitality of the present-day retreat center, and the silence of the wilderness mingle at Holden, making a visit memorable.

The tailings from the Holden Mine, rusted to a bright orange, were a jarring site against the natural colors of their wilderness background before the rehabilitation project. PAUL HART, JR.

The Wenatchee National Forest offers hundreds of miles of rushing mountain streams like Nason Creek, a tributary of the Wenatchee River. The valley of Nason Creek provided part of the cross-Cascades route for the Great Northern Railway in the 1890s. PAT O'HARA

ponderosa pine grow along the road near the campground, but they are dwarfed by giant Douglas-fir, true fir, and white pine down in the campground. A stroll on the trail along the river reveals that cottonwoods can grow almost as large in diameter as redwoods.

As if big trees weren't enough, across the road from the campground a trail leads to Silver Falls. This 175-foot waterfall changes moods with the seasons. In the spring it roars and sprays its admirers with mist. In the summer and fall the roar is muted, and it gracefully drapes its cliff with a curtain of water. Winter entombs the falls in ice, but faint sounds of falling water can still be heard deep within this seven-story icicle.

South of the Entiat Valley, several major highways

A Forest Service employee inspects a ponderosa, or yellow, pine — one of the primary conifers of the east slopes of the Cascade Range. The bark looks like layers of little jigsaw puzzle pieces and gives off a fragrant vanilla smell on warm days.
JACK C. WHITT

cross the forest from east to west, each providing enough scenic drives, trails, views, fishing holes, berry-picking, and campsites to keep a visitor busy for many years.

For example, a trip westward into the national forest on U.S. Highway 2 begins at the town of Leavenworth, a replica of a Bavarian village. A side trip on Forest Road 7600, known as Icicle Road, winds along a river rushing among house-sized boulders below towering granite cliffs. The twenty-mile road offers seven campgrounds, numerous trailheads, fishing, and excellent rock climbing before it ends at the edge of the Alpine Lakes Wilderness.

Back on Highway 2, headed west out of Leavenworth, travelers enter the mouth of Tumwater Canyon. For a dizzying few miles, the road parallels the Wenatchee River as it twists, turns, tumbles, and falls. Snowmelt swells the river each spring into a fearsome spectacle of raging whitewater. River watchers at overlooks must shout to be heard above the roar.

Mountains surround Lyman Lake in the Glacier Peak Wilderness. The lake is the headwaters of Railroad Creek, which flows past Holden Village and into Lake Chelan. Those who camp at Lyman Lake can spend weeks exploring surrounding passes, peaks, and glaciers. JOHN MARSHALL

During lower water in the summer and fall, anglers wade in the deep green pools between rapids, and climbers scale the sheer canyon walls.

At the western end of the canyon, Tumwater Campground welcomes weary travelers. Like most of the 150 campgrounds on the Wenatchee National Forest, it provides tent spots, tables, fire grates, pit toilets, and streamside rest for a small fee.

A few miles farther is the turnoff for Lake Wenatchee, a five-mile lake surrounded by thick woods and sheer mountain ridges. Private cabins and houses peek through the trees. Fishermen's boats dot the lake. On brisk, windy days, the bright sails of sailboards add color to the scene as windsurfers skim across the water.

The staff at the Lake Wenatchee Ranger Station can help plan an overnight hike into the Glacier Peak Wilderness.

A few hours of driving along the Little Wenatchee River Road brings hikers to the White Pass Trailhead. Thirteen miles of wilderness hiking and a gain of 4,000 feet in elevation bring hikers to White Pass, one of the most breathtaking spots in the North Cascades.

Summer hikers find fragrant blossoms of purple lupine, white valerian, and orange paintbrush along the trail and spread over hillsides. Ice-smothered Glacier Peak rises to the north, while the Pacific Crest National Scenic Trail wanders along the ridgetop. The trail can take hikers 2,000 miles south to Mexico or 200 miles north to Canada.

Highway 2 heading west also takes travelers to the

Stevens Pass Historic District. Interpretive signs at roadside stops tell the story of the 1890s construction of the Great Northern Railway over Stevens Pass and point out accessible sections of the railroad grade available for hiking.

As Highway 2 crests Stevens Pass, ski lodges appear along the road and ski lifts and runs stripe the hillsides. Like the six other ski areas on the Wenatchee National Forest, the Stevens Pass Ski Area operates on

A bull elk blends in with the trees, left. Elk, along with deer, bear, and grouse, provide hunting opportunities for thousands of hunters each fall on the Wenatchee National Forest.
DON ERICKSON

Skiers glide down the slopes at the Stevens Pass Ski Area, below, located at the crest of the Cascades on the boundary between the Wenatchee and the Mount Baker-Snoqualmie national forests. JOHN MARSHALL

A prairie falcon perches for a moment, left. Prairie falcons live in the canyons and on the open lower slopes of the east side of the Cascades, preying on small birds and rodents. They resemble their more famous raptor cousin, the peregrine falcon. ART WOLFE

leased national forest land and welcomes hundreds of thousands of skiers from November to April each year. Most come from the urban areas of Puget Sound, a two-hour drive to the west.

Winter draws other recreationists, as well. Many snowshoers, cross-country skiers, and snowmobilers travel farther east to enjoy the winter sunshine in the Wenatchee National Forest.

People from western Washington travel over the passes to the Wenatchee forest during other seasons, as well. They escape April gray skies by driving over Snoqualmie Pass on Highway 90 to the spring sunshine of the Cle Elum

The autumn oranges, reds, and yellows of deciduous trees contrast with the somber, never-changing greens of the conifers to make a striking design on Nason Ridge. PAT O'HARA

National forest visitors who keep an eye on the ground may spy rock lilies in the Columbia River Basin. PAT O'HARA

district. Here they will find some of the nation's largest and most popular campgrounds near Lake Kachess and Lake Cle Elum. They can explore Table Mountain, a sprawling subalpine plateau north of Ellensburg, and glimpse elk grazing in meadows fringed with conifers and aspen.

Or they can trade October drizzle for crisp autumn blue skies by driving the spectacular Mather Memorial Parkway eastward over Chinook Pass to the Naches district. The parkway, which passes through two national forests and Mount Rainier National Park, is named for the first National Park Service director, Stephen Mather.

The road descends along the American River into the Wenatchee National Forest in a narrow motorized corridor between two roadless wildernesses — Norse Peak to the north and William O. Douglas to the south.

The Union Creek trailhead is an example of stops available along the road.

Kayakers beach their craft during a whitewater rodeo on the Wenatchee River. The river's boiling rapids provide challenges for water enthusiasts. PAT O'HARA

WHEN FIRE HITS A FOREST

The Wenatchee National Forest knows fire. The very few inches of rain that fall during the hot summer usually come from thunderstorms. When lightning strikes tinder-dry trees, fire almost always results.

Hundreds of acres burn on the national forest every summer. Some years are worse than others. In 1970, more than 400 fires blackened 122,000 acres on the Wenatchee National Forest, which is known nationally as a "fire forest."

Most pine forests of the Wenatchee National Forest burned naturally every twenty to thirty years before the Forest Service began subduing the blazes in the twentieth century. And fire actually benefits some species by allowing new growth and controlling disease.

For example, Thompson's clover, with its big-headed purple blossoms, grows back more thickly after a fire.

Lodgepole pine often sprout after forest fires, as well, because the heat of the flames melts the resin that seals the pine cones. The cones then pop open and release seeds.

Most forest fires are caused by lightning. Others are caused by still-burning campfires or cigarettes, sparks from hot exhaust systems, or flames from burning debris piles on private land.

Forest Service fire patrols, lookouts, recreationists, or private pilots usually report fires quickly. When a fire is located, firefighters are dispatched to put it out. The first firefighters may arrive by road, but two-thirds of the forest is roadless. In isolated areas, the initial crews are often smokejumpers parachuting

When a forest fire "blows up" in the wind, it flares into the crowns of the trees and and spreads so fast that it often rages out of control.
CHRISTIE FAIRCHILD

from an aircraft or rappellers sliding down ropes from a hovering helicopter.

Because of the rugged terrain of much of the Wenatchee National Forest, one of the nation's few helicopter rappelling bases is located at the Chelan Airport. A ten-person crew of experienced firefighters receives intensive training in rappelling and in tactics for attacking fires in steep, remote terrain.

If the wildfire escapes the first attack, an army of firefighters and additional aircraft are mobilized. More than 12,000 people from all over the nation fought the 1970 Wenatchee National Forest fires over a five-week period.

Some of the yellow-shirted firefighters are men and women from the Wenatchee National Forest, borrowed from their regular jobs. Some crews come from other national forests in Washington and Oregon. And if the fire is large enough, firefighters are called in from other regions of the United States. Because fires know no property lines, Forest Service firefighters often work shoulder-to-shoulder with crews from the Washington Department of Natural Resources, National Park Service, Bureau of Land Management, Bureau of Indian Affairs, and rural fire departments.

Fire lines are the first tactic in fighting the blazes. The crew uses handtools to dig a trail across the leading edge of the fire and stop the advancing flames. Burning trees near the line are cut down. Hoses are laid to subdue flames with water and wet down unburned wood. Water may be pumped into the hose system from a tanker truck or fire engine or from a nearby creek, lake, or pond.

Meanwhile, other crews are sent to the scene, and bulldozers are used to excavate wide firebreaks in areas accessible to machinery. Planes drop fire retardant and helicopters drop water on hot spots and the fast-moving front of the fire.

Rain or snow sometimes helps the firefighters finally put out the fire. With the last embers snuffed, the camp comes down, crews go home, and Wenatchee National Forest employees return to everyday tasks — until the next thunderstorm.

Liquid fertilizer dropped from planes slows fires by cutting off oxygen to the flames. Planes and helicopters also drop huge buckets of water on particularly hot sections of a forest fire.
RICHARD MURRAY

Some plants like Thompson's clover need fire to thrive. This rare clover, found only in a small section of the Wenatchee National Forest, grows back with much more vitality after a fire.
PAUL HART, JR.

Spring rains bring color to the Columbia River Basin as phlox, lupine, and other wildflowers bloom among the sagebrush. The rest of the year, the basin is either too hot and dry or too cold and snowy for showy flowers to survive. PAT O'HARA

The quarter-mile trail leads to Union Falls, a series of foaming cascades flanked by serene woods that provide a cool, misty sanctuary on a hot summer day.

Farther down the parkway, a side trip to Bumping Lake beckons. Interpretive signs along the road to Bumping Lake introduce visitors to the late Supreme Court Justice William O. Douglas, a long-time summer resident of the village of Goose Prairie and a passionate wilderness advocate.

Bumping Lake, an irrigation reservoir for the Yakima Valley, covers the site of a natural lake used for thousands of years by Indians for salmon fishing, berry picking, and hunting. At one time the entire Wenatchee National Forest was Indian territory. The Yakima Tribe ceded the land to the U.S. government in the Wenatchee Treaty of 1855, but retained rights to traditional uses. The ceded lands became the Wenatchee National Forest in 1908.

On the trip back to the highway, visitors can take the Old River Road to visit Boulder Cave, a cavern in a lava flow. The mile-long trail is maintained to allow exploration of the cave by those with flashlights.

Off-road vehicle recreationists often take the next turnoff down the highway. The road up the Little Naches Valley takes them to the Old Naches Wagon Road, a pioneer trail that is part of the Wenatchee National Forest's extensive motorized trail system.

Below the Little Naches, the highway leaves the national forest and travels on into Yakima. But Forest Road 1500 turns south off the highway, re-enters the national forest, and meanders to U.S. Highway 12, another major east-west route across the Cascades. Here travelers can loop back to the west side of the mountains by driving west, up and over White Pass.

Visitors traveling to White Pass past Rimrock Lake could look at the ridge south of the lake and never know it was logged by helicopter in the 1980s. The timber harvest units were so carefully located that they are almost invisible

The Napeequa Valley in the Glacier Peak Wilderness has been called the Shangri-La of the North Cascades, because of its isolation and lush beauty. SCOTT PRICE

from the road. This timber sale is one of many examples of how Forest Service resource managers meet the need for wood products while preserving scenic views.

Balancing forest uses other than timber harvest and recreation also challenge Wenatchee National Forest managers. They must decide such questions as whether mining should be allowed along a stream with an endangered bull trout population or whether firewood cutters may work during high fire danger. They must even decide whether commercial mushroom harvest will harm the delicate balances in forest soil.

A wide array of overlapping and sometimes conflicting forest uses requires high levels of training, commitment, and problem-solving ability from Wenatchee National Forest employees. Specialists including wildlife biologists, soil scientists, tree geneticists, recreation planners, and foresters work together to make decisions about the uses of the national forest.

Someone once said the Wenatchee National Forest has more of everything. It's hard to dispute that claim. From glaciers to sagebrush, from mountain goats to rattlesnakes, from wilderness to clearcuts, from ecologists to engineers, this national forest helps define the word "diversity." ∎

Gnome Tarn in the Enchantment Basin doubles the stark lines of Prussik Peak with a reflection in the morning light. Enchantment Basin is part of the Alpine Lakes Wilderness. PAT O'HARA

WENATCHEE
NATIONAL FOREST DIRECTORY

POINTS OF INTEREST

LAKE CHELAN lies within an eighty-mile glacial valley near the center of the state. Rolling hills at the southern end contrast with the spectacular fjord-like quality at the northern end. This major recreation area contains several Forest Service campgrounds.

PACIFIC CREST NATIONAL SCENIC TRAIL travels the length of the national forest, passing through spectacular alpine scenery within six wilderness areas. A total of 153 miles of the 2,500-mile Mexico-to-Canada route are within the Wenatchee National Forest.

WILDERNESSES

LAKE CHELAN-SAWTOOTH 56,456 acres on the Wenatchee contain rocky canyons, jagged peaks, and large wildflower meadows.

GLACIER PEAK 289,234 acres on the Wenatchee, with numerous active glaciers. Glacier Peak, a dormant volcano reaches to 10,541 feet.

HENRY M. JACKSON 27,242 acres on the Wenatchee include easy day hikes to mountain lakes as well as a popular portion of the Pacific Crest National Scenic Trail north of Stevens Pass.

ALPINE LAKES 246,330 acres on the Wenatchee include 800 miles of trail over a landscape sprinkled with more than 700 small mountain lakes. Permits required for entry into the popular Enchantments area.

NORSE PEAK 51,364 acres on the Wenatchee straddle the Cascade crest between Chinook and Naches passes.

WILLIAM O. DOUGLAS 152,408 acres on the Wenatchee include hundreds of small lakes and tributaries for four major rivers: the American, Bumping, Little Naches, and Tieton.

GOAT ROCKS 36,333 acres on the Wenatchee, with many volcanic features. Mountain goats can be found near Bear Creek Mountain.

RECREATIONAL OPPORTUNITIES

HIKING AND RIDING Hikers and horses can use more than 2,600 miles of trails, 48 percent of which are within wildernesses.

CAMPING Approximately 150 campgrounds and picnic areas. Dispersed camping is allowed on most of the national forest.

SCENIC DRIVES 4,700 miles of roads winding through a variety of scenery. Major highways cross several mountain passes within the national forest, providing different panoramas with the changing seasons.

RAFTING, KAYAKING, AND CANOEING Several rivers offer whitewater, including the Wenatchee, White, and Tieton. Rushing waters, rocky runs, and logjams require expert skills or experienced guides.

HUNTING Known throughout the state for fine elk hunting. Hunters also pursue mule deer, black bear, and upland birds.

FISHING 241 lakes and reservoirs and 1,769 miles of streams and rivers. Game fish include coho, sockeye, and kokanee salmon, several varieties of trout, and burbot, smallmouth bass, largemouth bass, and yellow perch.

ALPINE SKIING Mission Ridge Ski Area (four chairlifts and two rope tows), thirteen miles from Wenatchee; Stevens Pass Ski Area (eight chairlifts), thirty-five miles east of Leavenworth; Snoqualmie Pass ski areas (four areas with a total of twenty-two lifts), approximately fifty miles east of Seattle; White Pass Ski Area (four chairlifts and one rope tow), sixteen miles east of Packwood.

CROSS-COUNTRY SKIING 120 miles of maintained, signed cross-country ski trails on the national forest. Snow-covered roads and open terrain provide many additional miles of skiing.

SNOWMOBILING Thousands of miles of snow-covered roads are available for snowmobiling each winter, along with 450 miles of groomed trail.

OFF-ROAD VEHICLE USE All national forest roads are available for four-wheel-drive vehicles. Nearly 800 miles of trail are open to motorbikes and pedal-powered mountain bikes.

ADMINISTRATIVE OFFICES

FOREST HEADQUARTERS Federal Building, P.O. Box 811, Wenatchee, WA 98807 (509) 662-4335

CHELAN RANGER STATION 428 W. Woodin Ave., Chelan, WA 98816 (509) 682-2576 or (509) 664-2702

CLE ELUM RANGER STATION West 2nd, Cle Elum, WA 98922 (509) 674-4411

LAKE WENATCHEE RANGER STATION Star Route, Box 109, Leavenworth, WA 98826 (509) 664-2704

LEAVENWORTH RANGER STATION 600 Sherbourne, Leavenworth, WA 98826 (509) 782-1413

NACHES RANGER STATION 10061 Highway 12, Naches, WA 98937 (509) 653-2205 or (509) 664-1719

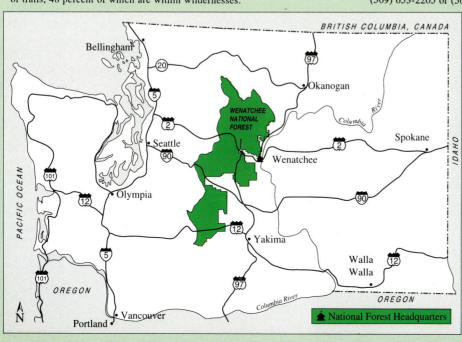

The ragged spires of Silver Star Peak glow in low-angle sunlight just east of Washington Pass on the North Cascades National Scenic Highway in the Okanogan National Forest. PAT O'HARA

Okanogan
N A T I O N A L F O R E S T

A land along the border

Lynx don't care if their snowshoe hare dinner is from Canada or the United States. Rivers pay little attention to international borders. And rocks certainly don't change chemistry depending on their national origin.

The Okanogan National Forest in northcentral Washington shares its seventy-mile northern border with Canada. Many rock formations and ecosystems cross the line. Streams and weather flow from one country to the other. Animals rarely found in Washington — moose, wolves, and grizzly bears — migrate back and forth between Canada and the Okanogan National Forest.

For at least two million years, even larger things have crossed the border. Continental ice sheets, a mile thick and hundreds of miles wide, surged south several times during the Ice Age, covering almost every surface with glaciers. The shapes of the peaks and valleys, the soil, and even some species of plants and animals are legacies of this Canadian ice.

Today, the Okanogan River continues to bring change from the north. The river flows south out of Canada and carves the valley that divides the Okanogan National Forest in two. East of the river, the national forest covers the forested tops of rolling hills known as the Okanogan Highlands. West of the river, it spreads over the eastern slopes of the Cascade Range as far south as Lake Chelan.

Visitors also come from Canada, usually driving south on U.S. Highway 97 and turning off the highway into the Okanogan National Forest at the towns of Tonasket or Okanogan. Visitors from the United States travel from the south on Highway 97 or from the east or west via Washington Highway 20, designated the North Cascades National Scenic Highway where it crosses the Cascade Range.

The highest portions of this highway usually are open only from April to November. In winter, avalanches thunder off the peaks and bury the road with snow. When the highway opens each spring, it provides

The immense rock towers of Liberty Bell Mountain impress visitors at the Washington Pass Overlook, a stop at the high point of the North Cascades National Scenic Highway. Liberty Bell is one of many impressive mountains visible along this drive across the Cascade Range. LARRY ULRICH

a direct and scenic route to the Okanogan National Forest from large cities on the west side of the Cascades.

Those driving east on the North Cascades National Scenic Highway pass through the Mount Baker-Snoqualmie National Forest and Ross Lake National Recreation Area, part of the North Cascades National Park Complex, before entering the Okanogan National Forest as the road climbs toward passes at the crest of the mountains.

At 4,000-foot Rainy Pass, a flat, paved, barrier-free trail leads to Rainy Lake. This area also provides access to the Pacific Crest National Scenic Trail,

Rainy Creek rushes past snow-dusted fir trees near Rainy Pass, along the North Cascades National Scenic Highway at the western edge of the Okanogan National Forest. LARRY ULRICH

Tiny bell-shaped blossoms of pink heather grace the sides of boulders in this timberline meadow at the headwaters of the Methow River. PAT O'HARA

which runs north to Canada and south to Mexico.

Farther east at mile-high Washington Pass, a quarter-mile overlook trail also is paved and barrier-free. The overlook provides views of the granite fingers of Early Winters Spires and 7,720-foot Liberty Bell Mountain.

As visitors start down the east side of the mountains, they see a transition from thick fir and hemlock forests to more open stands of ponderosa and lodgepole pine and interior Douglas-fir. Pine and Douglas-fir forests dominate the Okanogan National Forest, because the eastern slopes of the mountains receive plenty of sun and only moderate amounts of rain.

Much of the weather here comes from the Pacific Ocean. Saturated clouds blowing in from the west drop most of their moisture as they rise over the west slopes of the Cascades. Areas near the crest receive as much as 120 inches of precipitation per year. The more eastern, drier parts of the national forest receive just eighteen inches of moisture a year.

Roadcuts on the North Cascades National Scenic Highway showcase some of the core rocks of the Cascade Range. Veins of white quartz crisscross darker rocks like spider webs. These rocks have been pressure-cooked in the depths of the earth and then shoved upward with the mountains.

Glaciers carved the craggy spires that rise on either side of the highway. The granite peaks are part of the Goldenhorn Batholith, a huge molten mass of magma that welled up inside the rising Cascade Range and solidified underground. Millions of years of erosion have stripped away softer layers of rock that once covered the batholith, exposing the hard granite to its

ice sculptors.

When molten rock rose within the core of the Cascades it created more than future mountain peaks. Hot fluids, rich in minerals, migrated from the magma into cracks in the surrounding rocks. As these fluids cooled, gold, silver, and other minerals crystallized into mineral veins that later lured thousands of prospectors to the Cascades.

Visitors descending into the steep-walled Methow Valley on the North Cascades National Scenic Highway pass several campgrounds where an overnight stay allows time to fish the valley's streams or hike its trails. The scenic highway ends and the road becomes Highway 20 as it leaves the national forest near the town of Mazama. Travelers can continue on the main road into the towns of Winthrop and Twisp or take a side trip from Mazama to Hart's Pass.

The route to Hart's Pass is not for the faint of heart. The gravel road narrows to a single lane with a dizzying drop-off as it curves around Dead Horse Point. After twenty-three miles, the road ends in subalpine meadows at 7,500 feet, the highest road in the state of Washington. The parking area provides a 360-degree panorama of the Cascades, including views of Mount Baker and Glacier Peak. A few steps take hikers to the Pacific

Mushrooms unfurl their delicate caps above a bed of lacy moss on a rotting log, top. Fungi like these feed on decaying organic matter and play an important role in helping recycle nutrients back into the soil. PAT O'HARA

Autumn-touched aspen trees cling to a mountain slope in the Okanogan National Forest, left. Aspen leaves tremble when blown by the wind, thus the common name "quaking aspen." Aspen grow on the eastern slopes of the Cascades but are rarely found on the west side of the mountains.
RAY ATKESON

Crest Trail, into the Pasayten Wilderness, or up to the Slate Peak Lookout.

The U.S. Air Force tore down an old lookout and blasted off forty feet of Slate Peak's summit during the 1960s, to provide a platform for a radar station. It rebuilt the lookout on a tower, raising it forty-one feet, to fulfill its promise to the Forest Service that the new lookout would be as high, and have as good a view, as the old one.

Those who want a scenic drive with fewer precipices can try the Twisp River Road, which begins at the town of Twisp and meanders west along the Twisp River for more than twenty miles. Several small campgrounds provide riverside camping, especially popular with hunters during fall deer season.

The ruins of cabins in the Gilbert Mining Camp give the trip a historical flavor. At the road's end, visitors can look up at the impressive rock walls of Twisp Mountain and Lincoln Butte.

The War Creek Trail off the Twisp River Road is a portal to the Lake Chelan-Sawtooth Wilderness. This 95,976-acre wilderness covers the ridge between the Twisp River Valley and Lake Chelan Valley to the southwest. The War Creek Trail goes over this ridge and makes a great horseback trip, especially for those

Corral Creek rushes and gurgles between meadowed stream banks strewn with flowers in the Pasayten Wilderness. LARRY ULRICH

with time to spend a night on top.

After nine miles of moderate climbing, the trail reaches War Creek Pass and dips down into the Lake Juanita Basin, a meadowed dimple in the ridgetop. The trail then climbs from the lake to Purple Pass for views down to 55-mile Lake Chelan and the mountains beyond.

The Lake Chelan-Sawtooth Wilderness has no monopoly on horseback trips. The Pasayten Wilderness holds enough horse trails to keep a rider busy for months. The wilderness covers more than 500,000 acres of the northern Okanogan National Forest. Access to southern areas of the Pasayten Wilderness is

Most visitors are content to just look at the rock walls of Liberty Bell Mountain from the highway. An adventurous few challenge gravity on the vertical cliffs of the mountain, top. Only ropes, climbing hardware, and skill stand between each climber and a lethal fall. Those who climb say that the rewards outweigh the risks. ERIC SANFORD

Pack animals like these burros, below, help carry the gear for a Forest Service wilderness ranger in the Okanogan National Forest. Responsible packers carry feed for their stock and keep the animals out of streams and lakes. RICHARD MURRAY

ALWAYS READY TO GO

A siren wails over the quonset huts of the North Cascades Smokejumper Base near Winthrop. The twin engines of a plane roar to life. Eight smokejumpers leap into puncture-proof suits with parachutes attached. They stride to the aircraft and climb aboard. The plane accelerates down a runway, and its wheels leave the ground.

Only seven minutes have elapsed.

Smokejumpers must get to forest fires fast. They can prevent major fires by controlling lightning blazes before they spread beyond one or two trees. Everything at the North Cascades Smokejumper Base is designed to speed crews to fires as quickly and safely as possible.

All supplies are packed ahead of time and attached to the jumpsuits. Group gear such as chainsaws, first aid kits, and food are also prepacked, rigged with cargo parachutes, and stored aboard the aircraft.

As the plane makes its first pass over the fire, an experienced spotter in charge of the jump drops 200-foot crepe paper streamers. The whole crew watches as the yellow streamers flutter to the ground. The jump may be tricky if the streamers change direction when they hit low-level winds called "dirty air" or "burbles."

On the second pass, another set of streamers is released. If these land at the optimum jump spot, the third pass will be the real thing. The spotter signals to the first two jumpers, who hook their parachutes' static lines to a cable inside the open door. The spotter radios to the pilot, "Ready for jumper pass."

North Cascades smokejumpers climb aboard the plane that will take them to their next fire. They carry everything they may need for wilderness survival.
JIM HUGHES/PHOTOVENTURE

The plane circles and adjusts altitude to between 1,200 and 1,500 feet above the ground, low enough to minimize winds that blow parachuters off course and high enough so reserve parachutes can open if main parachutes malfunction. As the plane approaches the release spot, the spotter slaps the first two jumpers on the shoulders, and out they go.

The blue-and-white parachutes open immediately. These nylon canopies are thirty-two feet wide. With luck, a big, open landing spot waits below. Jumpers can steer with toggle cords, but if the trees are too close together the chute hangs up in the branches. Then the jumpers must rappel down the tree using long ropes included in their gear.

The first jumper, or incident commander, checks out the fire on the ground and radios to the spotter if additional jumpers or supplies are needed. After everyone and everything is on the ground, the hard work of digging fire lines, cutting down burning trees, and "mopping up" smoking debris begins.

After the fire is out, the crew is picked up by helicopter or walks back to the nearest road carrying 100-pound packs. These journeys can be more than twenty miles long, sometimes without a trail. The smokejumpers then return to the base to get ready for the next fire call.

Although located on the Okanogan National Forest, the smokejumpers serve as firefighting resources for the entire nation. If the North Cascades crew is on a fire in Alaska or Arizona, crews from other bases transfer to the base as backup. During an average fire season, jumpers dispatched from the North Cascades Smokejumper Base parachute on more than 100 fires in Washington and Oregon.

from Mazama or Winthrop. The northern and eastern parts are reached via the town of Tonasket.

The Horseshoe Basin Trail, which begins twenty miles northeast of Tonasket, is one of the easiest ways for riders and hikers to reach the miles and miles of rolling meadows of the eastern Pasayten Wilderness. At the end of the easy, five-mile trail, campsites and stock forage abound in a huge, bowl-shaped meadow ringed with clusters of trees and rocky peaks.

The Boundary Trail passes through Horseshoe Basin as it traverses the northern part of the wilderness for more than seventy miles, mostly above timberline. Side trails off the Boundary Trail lead to countless wilderness nooks and crannies where a person can spend days in solitude.

When the first November avalanche closes the North Cascades National Scenic Highway, the Okanogan National Forest regains some of the isolation it knew before the road was built in 1972. Snowmobilers and skiers replace the horseback riders and hikers along snowbound forest roads.

The Methow Valley has been called the cross-country skiing center of the Pacific Northwest. The Methow Valley Ski Touring Association grooms more than seventy miles of trails on the national forest. Skiers pay a fee for each day of skiing, to help support maintenance of trails and parking areas.

Novice skiers can try their skills on easy trails over flat and rolling farm and woodlands. The more advanced can follow professional guides into the mountains for overnight trips or extended tours or ride a helicopter up to really challenging terrain.

A series of European-style backcountry huts on national forest land provides rustic overnight accommodations. Gear is packed from hut to hut in snowmobiles with sleds, while guests ski free of heavy backpacks.

A downhill ski area with chairlifts and rope tows operates on the national forest at Loup Loup Pass between Twisp and Okanogan. This small, family-oriented ski area provides runs for skiers of all abilities amid rocky summits and ponderosa pine forest.

The Okanogan National Forest has fed, clothed, and housed people for more than 5,000 years. Indians knew these mountains contained riches: meat, berries, and fish. Several tribes used the area seasonally, and some

Heliskiing takes the adventurous to pristine slopes far back in the mountains. Experienced guides remove much of the risk, but avalanches and foul weather still present enough danger to keep adrenaline flowing. ERIC SANFORD

Mule deer bucks spar in the fall during breeding season, right. Although the male deer compete with their antlers for females, they rarely fight to the point of injury.
TOM AND PAT LEESON

Wildflowers give color to the hills of McCall Gulch, in the Pasayten Wilderness, below. The gulch and nearby Dollar Watch Mountain probably earned their names during the mining boom at the turn of the century. LARRY ULRICH

lived year-round in the mountain valleys. They gave the area its first names: Twisp, Methow, Pasayten, Chewuck, and Okanogan.

Miners came in the late 1800s in search of other riches, following fur trappers who told of gold in the Cascades. The place names from their era reflect their purposes: Copper Creek, Gold Ridge, Topaz Mountain. They probed almost everywhere in the mountains with their picks and shovels and found the minerals left by the rising magma.

Thousands of mining claims were filed in the area by 1900. But like most Cascades mines, few deposits were concentrated enough to be profitable. By World War I, the mining boom had faded, and few mines remained in operation. Short tunnels, collapsed shacks, and pieces of rusted machinery can still be found on the Okanogan National Forest, reminders of the era of Cascade gold fever.

Modern exploration and extraction technology brought miners back to the Okanogan National Forest in the 1980s. The Okanogan and Wenatchee have the most active mining claims of the state's national forests. Mining legislation passed by Congress in 1872 still encourages prospecting on national forests. Backed by big mining companies, some modern prospectors have been able to look deeper and longer than their earlier counterparts. Claims in the eastern part of the forest are proving rich enough to justify commercial mining.

Miners today submit a plan to the Forest Service outlining how they will minimize environmental damage and rehabilitate the land surface after mining. The Forest Service evaluates alternatives for access and environmental protection. The public provides comment by expressing views at public meetings.

In the early days, miners had to dig and blast to make a discovery, and only found ore near the surface. Today's prospectors often use non-disturbing scientific techniques to locate hidden deposits overlooked in earlier eras. Miners no longer build roads into the national forest to explore for minerals. They prospect on foot or via helicopters. Roads are built only after a claim has been proved viable.

The Okanogan also is used by ranchers, who graze their sheep and cattle in the Pasayten and Lake Chelan-Sawtooth wildernesses and throughout most of the national forest under grazing permits. It's possible to walk around a curve in the trail and come upon several thousand sheep on a hillside.

The historic tradition of sheepherding in the Okanogan National Forest continues today. A band of sheep, above, grazes on a national forest meadow. The national forest lands support several thousand sheep each summer. RICHARD MURRAY

National forest lands are used for a number of economic activities, including logging. But the Forest Service figures a number of environmental factors into each timber harvest decision it makes. LARRY MAYER

75

MANAGING TIMBER FOR HABITAT NEEDS

Wild cats with tufted ears and very large furry feet live in the Okanogan National Forest. Lynx — a longer-legged relative of the bobcat — range south from Canada, hunting for their favorite food, snowshoe hare. The Okanogan National Forest may have the largest concentration of lynx in the continental United States.

Part of the national forest has been set aside as a lynx habitat area. Within these several thousand acres of timbered ridges between the Okanogan and Methow valleys, the needs of lynx and snowshoe hare determine when, where, and which trees will be harvested.

Unlike more opportunistic large predators such as cougar, lynx primarily feed on one species — snowshoe hare. Studies of lynx and snowshoe hare populations in Canada show that when the hare population peaks every six to ten years, the lynx population also peaks. When hare numbers plummet after the peak year, lynx numbers also decrease rapidly.

What is good for snowshoe hare is good for lynx. And snowshoe hare thrive in dense young stands of lodgepole pine. The hare eat the bark and cambium layer of pines

Lynx differ from most wild North American cats in that they rely almost exclusively on one food source, snowshoe hare. JEFF MARCH

that are less than twenty years old. They feed in the dense cover of small trees growing close together. These thick stands of young lodgepole typically grow after forest fires.

Lynx populations on the Okanogan National Forest seem to be in trouble. Numbers are low, and kitten survival is poor. During good years in prime habitat, 80 percent of the young survive. Recently on the Okanogan National Forest, less than 20 percent of the kittens have survived.

Scientists speculate that fire suppression efforts have reduced the amount of young lodgepole pine in the Okanogan National Forest. With less habitat available, snowshoe hare populations probably have declined. Lynx may be having

Grazing has been a traditional use of the high meadows since the turn of the century and was specifically included as an acceptable wilderness use when Congress passed the Wilderness Act in 1964. Permits limit the number of livestock in any given area. Grazing areas also are rotated from year to year, to reduce the effects on the meadows.

Timber harvest began in the area even before the Forest Service was established in 1905. Forest management has changed dramatically since miners and homesteaders cut those first trees to build their cabins. Each year, research has revealed more about the complexity of forest ecosystems, and Forest Service managers have added more factors to their timber harvest decisions.

Today, some areas are managed for the needs of wildlife such as wolves, lynx, or grizzly bear. Resource harvest must enhance, or at least not harm, wildlife habitat. In other areas, sensitive plants, visual resources, or recreation uses must be protected if trees

difficulty finding enough food to survive and reproduce.

So managers on the Okanogan National Forest have come up with a way to avoid the dangers of wildfire, by using timber harvests to duplicate the role of fire in the ecosystem.

Within the Okanogan's lynx habitat area, foresters are trying to meet the habitat needs of lynx and snowshoe hare while still providing timber for human needs. Minimal roads are built to stands of mature timber too old for snowshoe hare habitat. The trees are clearcut in patches less than 300 feet across because lynx will not travel across larger openings.

After harvest, the roads are closed, and the clearcuts naturally reseed with closely spaced lodgepole pine. Hare will not use the new lodgepole patches until they are ten to fifteen years old and will stop using them after the trees are about thirty to forty years old. Different areas must be harvested every few years in order to keep a portion of the forest at the right age for hare habitat.

Lynx feed in young lodgepole pine forests, but they den in large-diameter, old-growth spruce and fir forests. So Forest Service managers must also preserve old stands of trees with thick layers of rotting material on the ground, where lynx can hole up to have their kittens. These denning areas must be near the lodgepole feeding areas. Corridors of old-growth for lynx to travel between den habitat and hare habitat also aid lynx survival.

A mosaic of ecosystems emerges: clumps of old-growth and patches of young lodgepole pine connected by long, thin, old-growth travel corridors. It takes long-term, careful planning to design timber harvests to fit this pattern of optimum lynx habitat.

Lynx timber management is an example of how national forests are used for more than one purpose. In this case, lynx and humans both benefit from careful removal of just the right trees in just the right places at just the right times. Okanogan National Forest researchers continue to study lynx and other wildlife species to help plan timber harvest sensitive to habitat needs.

Snowshoe hare seem to mimic some of the features of their predator, the lynx. Both have large feet for travel on snow and large ears, possibly for hearing each other during the hunt. TOM AND PAT LEESON

are removed. Even in those parts of the forest where timber harvest is the primary goal, long-term forest health must be preserved.

The Okanogan National Forest sells millions of dollars worth of timber each year, supporting local economies and providing wood products for the nation. The timber harvest, which averaged about seventy million board feet in recent years, also adds to the federal treasury and to the state treasury to support schools. Teams of experts including ecologists, archaeologists, wildlife biologists, and foresters work together to reduce the effects of timber cutting on national forest ecosystems.

An impressive cadre of volunteers helps Forest Service employees care for the Okanogan National Forest. Unpaid hosts live in trailers or tents in most campgrounds during the summer, to provide information to visitors and maintain the toilets and campsites. These hosts are usually retired couples from various parts of the United States.

The Backcountry Horsemen of Washington help design and build horse camps, donating time, materials, and heavy equipment. They also maintain and clean trails and backcountry camps each year. Motorcycle and snowmobile groups also help maintain the trails their members enjoy.

Pacific Crest Outward Bound School volunteers spend many hours conducting site surveys to help determine whether backcountry areas are being damaged by overuse. The group then restores some areas to their natural state with revegetation.

Mentally disabled students from Omak High School volunteer in campgrounds on the Tonasket District. The students sand, repair, and paint picnic tables, clear and burn brush, and help with district recycling.

Young adults from such countries as Ghana, Germany, South Africa, Sweden, England, and Canada volunteer each year — through the Student Conservation Association and the American Hiking Association — to clean campgrounds and patrol wilderness trails.

These unpaid workers from abroad join with such natural forces as glaciers, rivers, weather, and wildlife in a tradition of crossing borders to bring international influences to the Okanogan National Forest. ■

Alpine lakes are tucked away among the peaks and meadows of the Pasayten Wilderness. Louden Lake is in Horseshoe Basin, a huge natural bowl of meadows located in the northeast corner of the Okanogan National Forest. CHARLES GURCHE

OKANOGAN
NATIONAL FOREST

POINTS OF INTEREST

WASHINGTON PASS SCENIC OVERLOOK, along the North Cascades National Scenic Highway (Washington Highway 20), provides spectacular views of Liberty Bell Mountain (7,790 feet) and Early Winters Spires. Interpretive services, a picnic area, a visitor information center, and a short loop trail to an overlook are suitable for wheelchairs. Highway 20 is usually open from late April through November.

HART'S PASS provides an unexcelled view of the North Cascades from 7,500-foot Slate Peak. The pass is a major trailhead for the Pacific Crest National Scenic Trail.

NORTH CASCADES SMOKEJUMPER BASE, four miles south of Winthrop on County Road 9129, is the birthplace of the Forest Service smokejumper program. Visitors are welcome to tour the base during the summer.

GILBERT is a turn-of-the-century mining camp along the Twisp River that once had a population of 1,500. Two cabins and remains of others still can be seen.

BIG TREE BOTANICAL AREA is one mile northeast of Lost Lake on the Tonasket Ranger District. It's an easy fifteen-minute hike to large specimens of native western larch trees.

WILDERNESSES

PASAYTEN 529,850 acres stretching along the Canadian border in the northern part of the national forest. Many miles of maintained trails are open to hikers and horseback riders.

LAKE CHELAN-SAWTOOTH 95,976 acres of rugged and steep subalpine and alpine zones above 6,000 feet. Many alpine lakes nestle in the crags.

RECREATIONAL OPPORTUNITIES

HIKING AND RIDING More than 1,500 miles of trails, mostly within the two wildernesses, are open to foot and horse travel.

CAMPING Thirty-nine campgrounds, located throughout the forest. Twenty have drinking water, garbage collection, and a fee. Free dispersed camping is allowed in most areas.

SCENIC DRIVES The North Cascades National Scenic Highway (Washington Highway 20) travels over Rainy and Washington passes, providing spectacular views and opportunities for short hikes. The Loup Loup Pass Highway (part of Washington Highway 20) provides a forty-minute scenic drive between Twisp and Okanogan.

RAFTING AND KAYAKING Good rafting and kayaking on the Methow River in early summer.

HUNTING One of the largest mule deer populations in the United States is located on the Okanogan National Forest. Upland bird and bear hunting are also popular.

FISHING Cutthroat and rainbow trout exist in most lakes and streams.

ALPINE SKIING Loup Loup Ski Bowl (one poma lift and one rope tow), seventeen miles west of Okanogan.

CROSS-COUNTRY SKIING The Methow Valley offers 150 kilometers of groomed ski trails, mostly on the national forest. Another fifteen miles of trails are groomed in the Havillah area, northeast of Tonasket.

SNOWMOBILING Thirteen Sno-parks, 370 miles of groomed trails, and numerous activities during the winter throughout the national forest.

MOUNTAIN BIKING The Methow Valley offers extensive mountain bike routes, plus hundreds of miles of national forest road.

OFF-ROAD VEHICLES The Twisp Valley offers motorbike trails in the Foggy Dew area and a few other areas. Check at the Twisp Ranger Station for locations.

ADMINISTRATIVE OFFICES

FOREST HEADQUARTERS 1240 S. Second, Okanogan, WA 98840 (509) 826-3175

TONASKET RANGER STATION 1 W. Winesap, Tonasket, WA 98855 (509) 486-2186

TWISP RANGER STATION 502 Glover, Twisp, WA 98856 (509) 997-2131

WINTHROP RANGER STATION W. Chewuch Rd., Winthrop, WA 98862 (509) 996-2266

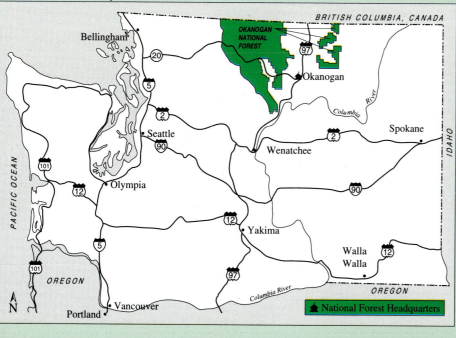

Goat Rocks Wilderness in the northeastern part of the Gifford Pinchot National Forest offers views of meadows, craggy peaks, and distant volcanoes such as Mount Adams. Mountain goats forage in the high meadows of the wilderness area during the summer. PAT O'HARA

Gifford Pinchot
N   A   T   I   O   N   A   L   F   O   R   E   S   T

A land of volcanoes

It's hard to avoid volcanoes in the Gifford Pinchot National Forest. Their white, glacier-capped summits seem to rise behind every ridge. First-time visitors to the jumble of hills and valleys within the national forest may lose their sense of direction and mix up the volcanoes. Old-timers soon learn the big mountains by their shapes.

Mount Adams, to the east, is flat-topped and bulbous, saddled with glaciers at the summit. Mount Rainier, to the north in Mount Rainier National Park, is drenched in ice and rises higher and swells wider than the others. Mount Hood, to the south in Oregon's Mount Hood National Forest, pokes the sky like a witch's hat. Mount St. Helens, to the west, is easy. It's the mountain with the insides blown out.

Almost every square inch of ground in the Gifford Pinchot National Forest was created by a volcano. Young lava flows show up as dark tongues of rock among the trees. Some poured from craters only a few hundred years ago and look as if they cooled yesterday. Older lava flows have resisted erosion to form peaks with names like Tower Rock and Steamboat Mountain.

Ash layers are more difficult to see, but they underlie almost everything that grows in the forest. A soil pit reveals layers of ash from many different eruptions over the course of hundreds of thousands of

years. This volcanic soil helps the Gifford Pinchot National Forest produce some of the fastest-growing trees in the world.

Prehistoric Indians knew about the volcanoes. Both the Klickitat and Cowlitz words for Mount St. Helens mean "fire mountain." An ancient ash-encased skeleton unearthed in a farmer's field near the forest in the 1930s suggests the tribes had reason to fear eruptions.

Indians have used the area for more than 10,000 years, a period in which volcanoes have erupted many times. After each eruption, people returned to a reshaped landscape. Some forests were destroyed, but new berry fields took their place. Some rivers might have been empty of fish, but deer would be thriving in new open areas. As plants and animals adapted to the changes, the Indians also adapted and continued to

Mount St. Helens National Volcanic Monument, left, offers interpretive programs at vista points, volcanic features, nature trails, and visitor centers.
JIM HUGHES

Trees grow well in the water-retaining ash left by volcanic eruptions, left. Much of the soil in the Cascade Mountains is made up of volcanic ash from the eruptions of numerous volcanoes over the last 10,000 years.
ROLAND EMETAZ

Mount St. Helens, far left, from the north displays evidence of the awesome power of volcanic eruptions. The once symmetrical, snowy peak is now a gray hollow shell. Trees were mowed down like blades of grass by the 1980 blast. JOHN MARSHALL

reap the bounty of this fiery place.

People continue to adapt today to changes wrought by volcanic eruptions. The 1980 eruption of Mount St. Helens was a vivid reminder that volcanoes in the Gifford Pinchot National Forest are alive and well.

Mount St. Helens blew off almost 1,000 feet of its summit in 1980. A wave of ash, gas, and steam three times hotter than boiling water roared north at speeds faster than a jet plane. The ash scorched or blew down 200 square miles of trees. Most of the dead trees still crisscross the hillsides like pick-up sticks. Fifty-seven people and countless animals lost their lives during the eruption.

Congress created the 110,000-acre Mount St. Helens National Volcanic Monument to preserve part of the blast zone. The Gifford Pinchot National Forest ad-

Climbers who reach the 8,365-foot rim of Mount St. Helens can look down into the huge crater left by the 1980 eruption. The Forest Service gives each climber instructions about what to do in case the volcano erupts. ROLAND EMETAZ

ministers the monument, and the land is altered only for recreation, education, and research. Within the monument, nature's healing processes work unaided and unfettered by humans.

A visit to the north and east sides of Mount St. Helens illustrates how natural forces destroy and renew landscapes. The yawning crater and the miles of desolate, gray blast zone contrast sharply with the snowy, graceful summit and lush forests of Mount St. Helens before the eruption.

Plants and animals are recolonizing the mountain's raw new face. Hummingbirds have hovered near geologists working in the steaming crater of the volcano. Pacific silver fir and mountain hemlock, buried in the snow during the eruption, survived and now seed surrounding areas. Elk graze in the weedy plants springing up among dead trees. Ten years after the 1980 eruption, almost every species that lived on Mount St. Helens before the blast had returned.

In the blast zone outside the Mount St. Helens National Volcanic Monument, plants and animals are also returning to old territories. People have returned with them, to harvest resources as they did before the eruption. Within two years of the eruption, loggers had salvaged most of the downed trees,

Roosevelt elk are returning to the 200 square miles of national forest land devastated by the eruption of Mount St. Helens. Public access and hunting has been restricted in some areas to help elk herds recover.
ROLAND EMETAZ

A black volcanic peak rises beyond a meadow dotted with fire-charred trees. This peak on Juniper Ridge has resisted erosion, helping the area earn the name "the dark divide." ALAN COSSITT

and Forest Service land managers had planted thousands of seedlings. Today, a new generation of trees is growing, and researchers are studying how ecosystems recover from eruptions with human assistance.

The 1980 eruption also changed the reputation of the Gifford Pinchot National Forest. Once known as a "working forest," the Gifford Pinchot produced the second-largest timber cut of any national forest in the United States. It was chosen in 1949 to bear the name of the first chief of the Forest Service, Gifford Pinchot, because it was such a good example of multiple use of public land.

But since the Mount St. Helens eruption, the Gifford Pinchot National forest has become one of the most popular attractions in the nation. Roads built for logging trucks are now as frequently used for scenic drives. Campgrounds once half-empty bulge at the seams. Visitors come from every state in the union.

Timber harvest and other commercial uses still occur in the forest, but recreation now plays a much more important role.

The Mount St. Helens Visitor Center near Castle Rock welcomes hundreds of thousands of visitors each year. Almost 10 percent come from other countries. The active volcano attracts them, but many stay longer than they intended or return for another visit once they discover the other recreational opportunities on the forest.

After stopping at the visitor center and viewing Mount St. Helens while driving along Windy Ridge, visitors can drive east through the national forest to camp on the shores of Takhlakh Lake, where Mount Adams rises in the background. Mount Adams, at 12,326 feet, is the second-highest volcano in Washington. Its western half lies within the Mount Adams Wilderness, one of seven wildernesses in the national

85

LENDING A HEALING HAND TO NATURE

The Clearwater Creek Valley isn't picture-postcard pretty. It was blasted by the 1980 Mount St. Helens eruption. Dead trees stick up like toothpicks along the ridgetops and in patches in the valleys. Road cuts and stream gullies on the hillsides are yellow-white with eroded ash.

But the banks of streams in the valley are green, and a close look reveals that most of it is covered with new growth.

The Clearwater Creek Valley lies outside the Mount St. Helens National Volcanic Monument. Thus the trees killed by the eruption could be harvested, producing enough wood to build 150,000 homes. Forest Service land managers have since replanted the land and are helping to speed the healing processes of nature.

Douglas-fir planted in the open sun and water-retaining ash are growing at phenomenal rates. Eighty percent of the seedlings planted in the early 1980s have survived. A single year's growth on some trees measures up to five feet. Some areas have ten-year-old trees that are twenty feet tall, growing so close together that they already need thinning.

The Forest Service planted willow, cottonwood, and red alder along streambanks to reduce erosion, cool the water for fish, and provide cover and forage for elk, deer, and smaller mammals. Fisheries biologists placed log sills and brush dams in creeks to create pools where sediment settles out and fish find still-water havens. Twenty-inch trout now swim in streams that once flowed with boiling mud.

Beaver returning to the valley have begun feeding on the streamside plantings. Some beaver have traveled all the way up to the headwaters of Clearwater Creek, at Meta Lake. Their dams have raised the level of the lake so that it floods the viewing deck and interpretive signs each spring.

Patches of dead trees have been left standing in the valley on purpose. They provide homes for cavity-nesting birds and mammals. The few living trees that survived the blast provide cover and diverse habitat for animals and a continual seed source for plant regeneration.

Research plots in the Clearwater Creek Valley have allowed scientists to compare growth rates of different species of trees with and without added fertilizer. Other plots have provided data about whether cards shielding seedlings from the sun help trees survive. A stream research plot has helped determine whether log jams in creeks aid fish survival.

In a sense, the Clearwater Creek Valley is one giant research project. In the future, efforts to help nature heal this valley will be compared to the results of the natural processes working alone within the Mount St. Helens National Volcanic Monument. The lessons learned here will help managers respond to the next eruption or other natural disaster that starts a forest over again.

Clearwater Creek flows off the northeastern slopes of Mount St. Helens. Most of the plants and animals in its valley were killed by the volcano's 1980 eruption. Today, life is returning to the valley, thanks to the healing processes of nature and the efforts of Forest Service managers and scientists. ROLAND EMETAZ

forest. The eastern half of the mountain falls within the Yakima Indian Reservation.

The Round the Mountain Trail circles Mount Adams at timberline. After toiling up one of the short, steep, access trails, hikers can stroll around the volcano for days. The Round the Mountain Trail travels through meadows, past lakes, and over rubbly lava fields. Horses and llamas are a common sight, as the Mount Adams trail system is open to pack stock.

With an ice axe, crampons, a rope, and some knowledge of glacier travel, scaling Mount Adams can be an exhilarating experience. Several hundred climbers each year start from the Round the Mountain Trail and ascend the many climbing routes up the glaciers and ridges of the mountain.

Climbers can also tackle the summit of Mount St. Helens during low volcanic activity. Numbers are limited during the summer and permits are required year-round. Climbers approach Mount St. Helens from the south, hike a trail through trees for a few miles, and then scramble up boulder-strewn ridges and snowfields to the rim of the crater. Those who reach the rim can look down at the lava dome growing within the huge crater.

Part of the extensive trail system outside wildernesses is open to mountain bike travel. In the winter, some trails are groomed for cross-country skiing and others for snowmobiling. Most forest roads offer opportuni-

Takhlakh Lake reflects the serene beauty of Mount Adams at sunset. Mount Adams is actually a cluster of volcanic cones. The oldest cone formed 450,000 years ago, while the most recent dates back 12,000 years.
RICK SCHAFER/RAY ATKESON PHOTOGRAPHY

The Lewis River flows from glaciers on the west side of Mount Adams and then travels around the south side of Mount St. Helens. The river cascades over a series of thirty-foot waterfalls before being captured by reservoirs downstream. ALAN COSSITT

Great fields of wild blueberries, also called huckleberries, grow in the national forest. Forest Service campgrounds near the fields host pickers overnight. ROLAND EMETAZ

ties to skiers and snowmobilers in the winter.

Visitors who prefer more sedentary pursuits will find plenty to do in the national forest. Signed interpretive trails, such as the Cedar Flats Trail or the Trail of Two Forests, take visitors on gentle walks through old-growth forests or along lava tubes created by eruptions of Mount St. Helens 1,900 years ago.

The 12,810-foot Ape Cave, the longest lava tube in the continental United States, is one example of the types of tunnels and caves that can form in cooling lava. It is open for exploration year-round. Guided interpretive walks and lantern rentals are available at Ape's Headquarters, along the road to the cave, in the summer.

Forest visitors who want a roof over their heads can reserve space at the Cispus Conference and Learning Center, near the town of Randle. Located at the site of an old Civilian Conservation Corps camp, the dormitories, houses, and classrooms provide a comfortable base camp from which to explore and learn about the surrounding "outdoor laboratory."

The Gifford Pinchot National Forest also has opportunities for those who like to take something home from their vacation. Fishing is good in the rivers and at the many lakes nestled among the lava flows. Hunting seasons are open for elk, deer, and other game species.

Huckleberry fields at the center of the national forest are famous. They've been used for thousands of years by several different Indian tribes. Tribal groups still visit traditional harvest areas such as the Sawtooth berry fields to pick the juicy blue berries during August and September.

Berries aren't the only crop on the national forest. Foragers can harvest bear grass, mushrooms, and firewood for home use, with a permit from one of the ranger stations of the national forest. Forest Service managers monitor harvest levels to maintain long-term health of the ecosystem.

Berry picking in the Sawtooth berry fields is often a visual as well as a culinary delight, especially when clouds lift to reveal the white summit of Mount Adams in the background. ALAN COSSITT

Whether visitors are picking huckleberries, climbing mountains, or driving forest roads, they are participating in a long tradition of human interaction with the lands of the Gifford Pinchot National Forest.

This history may be best illustrated at Layser Cave, an archaeological interpretive site a short drive from Randle.

From the mouth of the cave 7,000 years ago, ancestors of the Cowlitz Indians looked down upon the valley of the Cispus River and out at the summit of Mount Adams. What did they see? A clear cold, river choked with salmon each fall? A dense forest full of deer, elk, berries, and bark to be harvested for survival? An angry mountain god who hurled fire?

Today's view from the cave entrance is remarkably similar to that of 7,000 years ago. The river continues to run cold and clear. Anglers still catch salmon in its waters. Modern hunters carry on the tradition of stalking deer and elk. Berries and bark continue to grow, and foragers still harvest them. And the angry god still lurks within Mount Adams. Fire may yet come again from its snowy summit.

But much has happened in the last 7,000 years. Other parts of the national forest have been mowed down by lava flows or leveled by volcanic blasts. Fires have swept through some valleys and floods through

TREES FOR TOMORROW

Vibrant young seedlings grow in tidy rows in the Wind River Nursery tree beds. Nearly thirty species of trees are grown at the nursery. BOB AND IRA SPRING

Millions of baby trees sprout each year in the seed beds of the Wind River Nursery. Here they grow in the rich volcanic soil for two years until ready for transplanting. The seedlings become new generations of trees for national forests, state forests, and Indian tribal lands throughout the Pacific Northwest.

The nursery began in 1909, producing 99,000 trees each year on three acres of land. By 1990, it was producing twenty million seedlings a year on almost 200 acres. In the intervening eighty years, nursery managers, research scientists, and land managers learned many lessons about replanting forests.

Some of the first generations of trees at the nursery were eastern hardwoods. In 1912, the Forest Service established an experiment station at the nursery to work on such matters as improved nursery techniques and methods of reforestation.

Researchers planted about 200 species of hardwoods and conifers from around the world in the Wind River Arboretum. They wanted to discover whether species from other regions would do well in Pacific Northwest growing conditions.

The hardwoods were so unsuccessful that further study was abandoned in 1924. Many of the exotic conifers appeared more vigorous than local species at first. But after a few decades, the native trees continued to flourish, while most of the introduced species died or grew poorly.

Today's visitors to the Wind River Nursery can walk an

interpretive trail through the historic arboretum and see the withered remains of trees from Nepal, Norway, Scotland, and Siberia.

The Pacific Northwest Forest Experiment Station, located at the Wind River Nursery today, carries on the study of forests and how they thrive. Long-term research plots near the nursery include studies to answer such questions as how close together trees should be planted.

Many of the structures at the Wind River Nursery were built by the Civilian Conservation Corps (CCC) in the 1930s. These well-crafted and well-preserved historic buildings are now part of the nursery walking tour.

The tour also includes views of the Trout Creek Dam, a 32-foot-high concrete dam that, with its accompanying fish ladder, was the largest CCC project in the United States in 1935. The dam was built to provide electricity for the Wind River Nursery, research station, district, and CCC camp. The lake behind the dam was stocked with fish, and a picnic area was built along its shores.

The dam no longer generates electricity, but the lake provides water for irrigating seedlings in the Wind River Nursery, and visitors still enjoy the picnic area.

Today's Wind River Nursery is busy in every season. Cones arrive by the truckloads each fall, gathered by cone pickers around the Pacific Northwest. Each bag of cones is labeled with the species of tree and the location and elevation of the picking site. This information will follow the seeds throughout their life at the nursery. When each seedling is ready for transplanting, it will be returned to a site closely resembling the conditions of its parent tree.

The cone extractory is in full operation in the fall, removing seeds from cones and freezing them for long-term storage. In the spring, the seeds are soaked and softened to mimic spring rains. They then are planted in newly tilled ground. The seedlings in the outdoor beds and in the seventeen bedhouses used for early planting and accelerating growth are cultivated and fertilized in the summer. In the fall and spring, young trees ready for transplanting are lifted from their beds, graded, and packaged for shipment in the huge, automated warehouse of the tree processing center.

Modern forestry is now focusing on the long-term health and diversity of forest ecosystems, as well as on producing high volumes of timber. Thus the Wind River Nursery is beginning to grow species of trees that are important for uses other than wood products.

For example, cottonwood and alder seedlings from the nursery will be transplanted along streambanks denuded by volcanic eruptions, fires, or timber harvest. These riparian species provide cover and food for wildlife and reduce erosion and water temperatures.

The nursery also is exploring the propagation of Pacific yew trees. Yew bark contains a chemical called taxol, which has shown promise as a treatment for ovarian cancer. Bark from wild trees is being gathered for research purposes.

Visitors are welcome to watch almost every aspect of nursery operation. Guided tours are available with advance notice, and interpretive brochures and signs provide information about nursery functions and history.

Tree planters dig down to mineral soil to give young trees the best chance of survival. Each seedling is planted in an area similar to the environment from which its parent tree came. PAT O'HARA

others. Plants and animals and people have come and gone with cataclysm.

During the last 100 years, modern civilization has smoked and churned almost to the edge of the national forest. Roads, campgrounds, and clearcuts have brought their own types of change to the national forest, and ecosystems and people are adapting just as they adapted to changes that came before.

Walking in cathedral groves of 500-year-old trees within the national forest, it's hard to remember that active volcanoes reshape this land every few hundred years. The huge trees are taller than ten Tyrannosaurus Rex dinosaurs piled on top of one another. They seem eternal. Yet this forest grows where other forests have come and gone, and it too could someday be destroyed by eruptions.

The rushing waters of rivers on the Gifford Pinchot offer a number of whitewater rafting opportunities. Above, rafters shoot along the White Salmon River. DAVID SCOTT

Abundant rainfall and summer snowmelt feed countless clear streams that cascade through the dense forests of the Gifford Pinchot National Forest. The unnamed falls at left tumbles through lush greenery near Mount Adams. RAY ATKESON

The volcanoes that created the landforms, ecosystems, and human cultures of this national forest will continue to reshape them for eons to come. The underlying constants here seem to be change and adaptation to change. More than most national forests, the Gifford Pinchot National Forest is a land of continual endings and new beginnings. ∎

Alpine gardens bloom with abandon in the Goat Rocks Wilderness, above, each summer. Lupine, pink monkeyflower, and Indian paintbrush create a rich blend of colors and smells, making a walk through an alpine meadow a sensory delight.
PAT O'HARA

Large predators such as the bobcat, left, live in the wilder areas of the national forest, feeding primarily on small mammals like voles and rabbits. Bobcats are secretive and rarely seen by humans.
TOM AND PAT LEESON

GIFFORD PINCHOT
NATIONAL FOREST DIRECTORY

POINTS OF INTEREST

MOUNT ST. HELENS NATIONAL VOLCANIC MONUMENT is located east of Interstate 5 and can be reached by State Road 12, State Road 504, State Road 503, and State Road 14. The powerful eruption of the volcano on May 18, 1980, caused dramatic changes in the surrounding landscape. Congress created the 110,000-acre monument in 1982.

LAVA TUBES, CASTS, AND CAVES on the south side of Mount St. Helens were created by volcanic eruptions. Lava tubes and caves, formed in cooling lava, range from thousands of feet in length to small bubble-like chambers. Ape Cave, the longest known lava tube in the continental United States, has been developed for unguided exploration.

WIND RIVER NURSERY, in the southern part of the national forest, began growing seedlings in 1909, primarily to reforest lands after fire and timber harvest. Visitors are welcome to tour.

WILDERNESSES

GOAT ROCKS 71,670 acres on the Gifford Pinchot, in the northern part of the national forest. A rugged, beautiful land of flinty pinnacles, snowfields and glaciers, and wildflower meadows.

MOUNT ADAMS 47,000 acres on the western slopes of Mount Adams. The 12,326-foot volcano is the second-highest peak in the Northwest. Trails offer spectacular views of glaciers, tumbling streams, and wildflowers scattered among lava flows.

GLACIER VIEW 3,000 acres on the western boundary of Mount Rainier National Park. Outstanding scenic views.

INDIAN HEAVEN 20,600 acres of broad, rolling hills straddling the crest of the Cascades. An important area for local Indian tribes, the wilderness offers wildlife, panoramic views, wildflowers, and huckleberries.

TATOOSH 15,800 acres on the southern boundary of Mount Rainier National Park, including 550 acres of the Butter Creek Natural Area.

TRAPPER CREEK 6,000 acres ranging from old-growth Douglas-fir at lower elevations to rocky peaks, huckleberry fields, and high meadows.

WILLIAM O. DOUGLAS 15,880 acres on the Gifford Pinchot, containing scattered peaks, sharp ridges, steep slopes, and hundreds of small lakes.

RECREATIONAL OPPORTUNITIES

HIKING AND RIDING More than 1,000 miles of trail, including the Pacific Crest National Scenic Trail, range from flat interpretive loop trails less than a mile in length to high routes on Mount Adams and Mount St. Helens.

CAMPING AND PICNICKING Numerous camp and picnic grounds are available during the late spring, summer, and early fall. Dispersed camping is allowed in most areas of the national forest.

SCENIC DRIVES A number of one-day loop drives are possible. Contact the ranger stations for routes and suggestions.

RAFTING, KAYAKING, AND CANOEING The Cispus, Lewis, and White Salmon rivers offer early season floating opportunities. Contact ranger stations for suggestions.

HUNTING Black-tailed deer, Roosevelt elk, black bear, mountain goats, and grouse. Washington state fish and game regulations apply.

FISHING Streams and lakes harbor rainbow, brook, and cutthroat trout.

CROSS-COUNTRY SKIING Developed and undeveloped areas at Old Man Pass, Marble Mountain, White Pass, Mount Adams, and Mount St. Helens offer cross-country skiing.

SNOWMOBILING Available on forest roads and groomed trails including the Lahar and Lone Butte areas.

OFF-ROAD VEHICLES Trails and routes for mountain bikes, trail bikes, four-wheel-drive vehicles, and ATVs. Contact the Randle Ranger Station for suggestions.

ADMINISTRATIVE OFFICES

FOREST HEADQUARTERS 6926 E. Fourth Plain Blvd., P.O. Box 8944, Vancouver, WA 98668-8944 (206) 696-7500

MOUNT ST. HELENS NATIONAL VOLCANIC MONUMENT P.O. Box 369, Amboy, WA 98601 (206) 247-5473

MOUNT ST. HELENS VISITOR CENTER 3029 Spirit Lake Highway, Castle Rock, WA 98611-9719 (206) 274-6644

MOUNT ADAMS RANGER STATION Trout Lake, WA 98650 (509) 395-2501

PACKWOOD RANGER STATION Packwood, WA 98361 (206) 494-5515

RANDLE RANGER STATION Randle, WA 98377 (206) 497-7565

WIND RIVER RANGER STATION M.P. 1.46-R Hemlock Road, Carson, WA 98610 (509) 427-5645

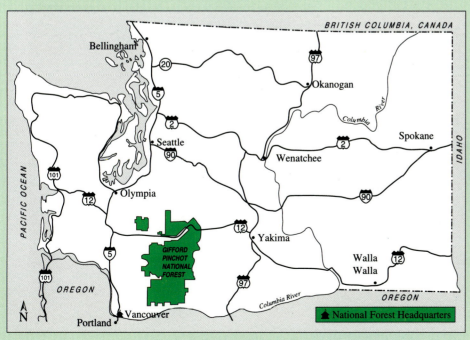

Peewee Falls plummets over a 200-foot vertical cliff into Boundary Dam Reservoir on the Pend Oreille River. This cascade on the Colville National Forest was originally named Periwee Falls in 1895 by a French-Canadian hunter and prospector. JIM LUTHY

Colville
NATIONAL FOREST

An overlooked treasure

The Colville National Forest disproves the widely held notion that Washington state lies flat east of the Cascade Mountains. These million acres in the northeast corner roll like the high seas. Three waves of mountains run from north to south, separated by troughs of valleys. These ranges — the Okanogan, Kettle River, and Selkirk — are considered foothills of the Rocky Mountains.

The troughs between the mountains channel water into the Columbia River system. The Pend Oreille River flows north into Canada to merge with the Columbia.

The major rivers in the national forest are following paths bulldozed by Ice Age glaciers. Mile-high ice sheets surging south from Canada drowned all but the tallest peaks several times during the last two million years. The ice ground off sharp edges, leaving the mountains well-rounded.

Today's landscape emerged from the melting ice about 10,000 years ago. Animals and plants followed the retreating glaciers northward, and humans were not far behind. The first Indians probably began hunting, fishing, and gathering in the area about 9,000 years ago.

And what a rich land it was! The new forests were full of deer, elk, and moose. Salmon swarmed in the rivers. Berries hung thick on the bushes. Camas bulbs ripened in the valleys. Kalispel tribal legend tells of scouts who once mistook a valley for a huge lake because it was so thick with blue camas blossoms.

Many tribes harvested the bounty, coming from as far away as Montana and Yakima during salmon runs. Tribes met each year at Kettle Falls on the Columbia River to fish and trade. Travel routes were worn into the ridgetops by centuries of yearly migration to the area.

Archaeologists estimate that Indians caught more than 1,000 salmon a day at Kettle Falls during peak runs. Salmon congregated below this wide, low falls on their way upstream to spawn. Fishermen stood on rocks and wooden platforms to spear and net the fish as they jumped up through the whitewater. People camping near the falls smoked and dried the fish, preserving it for winter use. Runners would carry the smoked fish back to the elders and young children who had remained behind in winter villages.

Some tribes stayed in the area year-round. The Kalispel wintered on the east banks of the Pend Oreille River. Kalispel means "camas people," and the tribe had territorial rights to some of the richest camas fields in the region. Camas bulbs provided much-needed carbohydrates to the diet of the Indians. Cooked in earth ovens, they tasted like sweet, smoky figs. Remains of ovens found today at the Pioneer Park archaeological dig along the Pend Oreille River date back more than 4,000 years.

Local tribes allowed other groups to harvest camas in exchange for goods such as obsidian from Yellowstone or shell necklaces from the Pacific Coast. They also traded camas for hunting privileges. The Blackfeet might come to the Pend Oreille Valley to dig bulbs, allowing the Kalispel to hunt buffalo in western Montana, in return.

The male western bluebird wears his bright plumage with pride as he perches on a pine branch, above. The female is paler and duller, while young birds are gray with speckled breasts.
TOM AND PAT LEESON

Camas opens its blue blossoms throughout the month of May, left. In large colonies, a few plants will have white flowers. The sweet, starchy bulb of the camas was a staple of early Indian diets. A variety of lily called "death camas," toxic to grazing animals, usually grows alongside true camas. MICHAEL S. SAMPLE

Autumn touches forests with color along the Pend Oreille River north of Spokane. The river flows north into British Columbia, Canada, where it merges with the Columbia River and then heads south, eventually to reach the Pacific Ocean near Portland, Oregon. JOHN MARSHALL

A rich spiritual tradition was interwoven with resource harvest. Many tribes welcomed the fish back to the river each year with a First Salmon Ceremony. Young people entering adulthood pursued vision quests in the mountains. The First Salmon Ceremony is still celebrated at an intertribal pow-wow at Kettle Falls each year, and modern young Indians spend days alone in the wilds of the mountains seeking to connect with their spiritual roots.

Changes to these seasonal routines came in 1809 with the arrival of the first non-Indian, fur trapper David Thompson, from Canada. The many trappers who followed were looking for beaver, marten, and other animal pelts to help satiate the European hunger for fur hats and coats. They traded with the Indians, introducing beads, tools, and alcohol to tribal culture.

Within a few decades, up to three-fourths of the Indians had died of illnesses to which they had no resistance, such as smallpox, tuberculosis, and measles. Missionaries had come to save Indian souls, and native religions were forced underground.

By 1826, American fur traders were living in Fort Colville, built near Kettle Falls. They brought in pigs and cattle, began farming around the fort, and limited

A pine marten peeks through the branches of an evergreen, top right. The animal is one of the most arboreal members of the weasel family. It has sharp semi-retractable claws for climbing and a long, bushy tail, about half the length of its body, that is used for balancing. Marten will eat squirrels, hares, and birds, but their main prey are mice and voles. ART WOLFE

The Kettle River Range spreads to the north in this view from the Kettle Crest, the divide between the Columbia and Pend Oreille rivers.
MIKE JAVORKA

Indian fishing access. By the late 1800s, the Indians were confined to reservations. Kettle Falls and the salmon runs disappeared under the rising waters of Roosevelt Reservoir in the 1930s, when Grand Coulee Dam was built.

Miners and homesteaders came around the turn of the century, each searching for riches in the mountains and valleys. Neither had much success. Gold and silver were found in the area around Republic but weren't plentiful elsewhere, and the growing season was short. The miners moved on to Alaska, and the homesteaders sold out to the government. By 1920, the population in northeast Washington was half of what it had been in 1910. Today, empty mines pock the hillsides, and rotting cabins stand in abandoned fields throughout the Colville National Forest.

Loggers and ranchers were more fortunate. They found good supplies of trees and grass on public land. Early land use was unregulated, but when the Colville National Forest was established in 1906, rangers began overseeing private resource harvest. After a hostile beginning, a working relationship evolved between the Forest Service and those who used the national forest lands.

The Civilian Conservation Corps changed the face of the Colville National Forest during the 1930s. CCC workers built roads, trails, camps, and buildings, many of which are still in use today. Camp Growden, known as "Little America" because it housed CCC enrollees from around the country, was built west of Kettle Falls. It was one of the largest CCC camps in the area. An octagonal concrete fountain and an earth-filled dam

Lodgepole pine grow on drier slopes in the mountains, often in crowded, single-species forests. The short, stout needles come in bundles of two. Lodgepole depend on fire to thrive. Some cones are so tightly sealed with resin that only the heat of fire frees the seeds. PAT O'HARA

A HIDDEN AND HISTORIC RETREAT

Tucked away in the hills east of Metaline Falls lies Sullivan Lake, a haven for visitors who relax at the area's summer cabins or Forest Service campgrounds.

People share the lake and the mountains that surround it with birds and wildlife. Loons, great blue heron, rednecked grebes, and mergansers feed and nest on the lake. Deer and bear roam the woods nearby. Hall Mountain, which rises on the east side of the lake, is home to a herd of not-so-wild bighorn mountain sheep.

Bighorn sheep probably ranged on Hall Mountain naturally until about 1900, when disease or unregulated hunting eliminated them. In 1972, the Washington Department of Wildlife released eighteen Rocky Mountain bighorns in an effort to re-establish a herd. The department now manages about sixty sheep near Sullivan Lake as a source of transplants to other areas in Washington.

Although the sheep could survive well on natural feed, they are fed each winter at the south end of Sullivan Lake so they will be available for research, veterinary treatment, and viewing. Hay is in the feeders at all times, and feed pellets are added once a week. Each spring, the feed is slowly reduced and finally eliminated, to encourage the animals to return to natural summer forage.

People often visit the feeders to get a close-up view of the bighorns, the largest sheep in North America. Rams can reach 300 pounds and grow thirty-pound horns.

The bald sides of Hall Mountain reflect in Sullivan Lake. Visitors staying in Forest Service campgrounds along the lakeshore can hike a seven-mile trail to the top of the mountain.
MIKE JAVORKA

The history of the Sullivan Lake area is summarized by interpretive signs along a mile-long, barrier-free trail at the Mill Pond, a mile down the road from Sullivan Lake. The trail passes ruined cabins and a five-seater outhouse to reach the slumped remains of the 2.5-mile wooden flume that used to carry water from Mill Pond to the town of Metaline Falls.

Sullivan Lake was raised forty feet in 1910 by a dam. Another dam on Sullivan Creek created Mill Pond downstream. A wooden flume, wide enough to drive a car through, provided water and electricity to the new cement plant and the town it spawned, Metaline Falls. This system of dams and flumes was a technological wonder in its day.

A boardwalk on top of the flume transformed it into a trail between Metaline Falls and Sullivan Lake. During the 1930s, Civilian Conservation Corps workers strolled the flume with their sweethearts to attend dances at the dancehall on the lakeshore.

The Civilian Conservation Corps era lives on at Sullivan Lake in the form of historic structures built by this government work program during the Depression. The Sullivan Lake Ranger Station is an example of the Cascadian style of architecture that became a hallmark of CCC projects.

The flume, the dancehall, and the CCC are just echoes of history now at Sullivan Lake. In most ways, the lake is less inhabited than in the past. Like most features in this corner of the state, Sullivan Lake could be described as undiscovered. Those few who find the lake today can experience a rare blend of rustic comfort and wildness.

Mist hovers over the lily pads of Nile Lake.
PAT O'HARA

still stand at the site. The Sullivan Lake and Newport ranger stations are CCC buildings, as are many of the fire lookouts on the national forest.

Resource harvest continues on the Colville National Forest today. Timber harvest remains one of the primary ways these lands meet economic needs. Because most of the national forest burned in the 1920s due to dry conditions and lightning strikes, a large crop of trees reached maturity in the 1990s. Thus, the Colville National Forest was able to harvest at high levels during an era when other national forests were severely reducing timber cutting.

Modern timber management differs markedly from the simple numbers control, slash burning, and single-species reforestation of the early years of the Forest Service. Today, foresters design timber sales to reduce environmental and visual impacts. Partial cuts are replacing clearcuts as the preferred harvest method. Live trees are left standing for natural seeding pur-

Volunteers install a new cedar shake roof on a cabin at the Mill Pond Historic Site near Sullivan Lake. The interpretive trail and restored buildings on the site were a cooperative effort between the Forest Service and many other agencies, organizations, and private individuals. MIKE JAVORKA

Western larch glow like burnished gold when their summer-green needles turn color after the first frosts. Although larch are conifers, they are not evergreen and they drop their needles each year. PAT O'HARA

poses, and standing snags are left for wildlife. Buffers of trees along rivers and lakes protect crucial riparian habitat for fish and wildlife.

The Colville National Forest is divided into management areas that have different emphases. For example, the primary objective in one area might be timber management, while wildlife needs or recreational opportunities might be the prime focus in other areas.

Reforestation has become a sophisticated science, and seed orchards on the Colville National Forest grow different genetic strains of "super trees." Researchers monitor tree growth and work to develop trees that are resistant to disease and adapt well to a wide variety of ecosystems.

Fire still affects timber management. The drier portions of the Colville burn naturally every twenty or thirty years. Even modern fire control methods are of little use when lightning strikes aged lodgepole stands after weeks of dry weather. The White Mountain Fire of 1988 burned more than 20,000 acres, reminding foresters that fire, as well as timber harvest, can start a forest over again.

Other natural resources also are harvested on the Colville. About 7,000 head of cattle graze on the national forest, allowing ranchers to grow hay on their private land during summer months. Permits are required, and no more than 50 percent of the available

Cattle graze in special allotments within the Colville National Forest, left. Using public lands for range allows ranchers to make hay of their own pastures, to feed the herds through the winter.
JIM HUGHES

Mature white-tail does and bucks, below, travel together only during the fall mating season. White-tailed deer share the mountains of eastern Washington with the larger mule deer. The whitetails tend to be found closer to settlements, while the mule deer prefer forest margins.
TOM AND PAT LEESON

105

The Salmo River flows through the rugged terrain of the Salmo-Priest Wilderness. TOM AND PAT LEESON

forage can be consumed by domestic livestock. The rest is preserved for wildlife.

Mining exploration, berry picking, firewood cutting, and other consumptive uses such as hunting and fishing still are permitted on national forest lands. In many cases, gathering forest products has become less a matter of economic survival and more a form of recreation.

Some of the best hunting in the state is on the Colville National Forest. About 60,000 of the state's estimated 90,000 white-tailed deer live in northeast Washington — a fact that has led to one of the longest deer hunting seasons and one of the highest success ratios in the nation.

Hunters also stalk elk in the national forest, and a few tags are sold by lottery for moose and bighorn sheep. The only moose hunt in Washington state occurs in Pend Oreille County in the very northeastern corner of the Colville National Forest. Each hunter can win only one moose tag in a lifetime.

Not everyone hunts with modern rifles. Archers and muzzleloader hunters have special seasons before and after the main hunting season. The archers ease quietly through the trees, their faces smudged with charcoal and their clothes colored camouflage green. Both they and the "black powder" muzzleloader hunters must get much closer to their prey than hunters with modern rifles. The success rate is much lower, but some say rewards are much greater for these hunters, who have relearned the skills of the pioneer past.

Not all wildlife can be hunted on the Colville National Forest. Mountain goat populations in the area are low, and these bearded, white members of the antelope family are protected in their rocky cliff habitat. Grizzly bear, caribou, and wolves all have been listed as threatened or endangered by the U.S. Fish and Wildlife Service. Recovery areas have been designated for both the grizzly and the caribou in the northeastern part of the Colville National Forest. A boggy meadow on the border between the Colville and Idaho Panhandle national forests even hosts a small population of northern bog lemmings.

The Salmo-Priest Wilderness offers a spot where hikers can see all kinds of wildlife and few people. Located on the wet, west slopes of the Selkirk Mountains, this wilderness contains huge old redcedar, Douglas-fir, and western hemlock. Living in the old growth and in the meadows and crags above are grizzly and black bear, cougar, caribou, elk, deer, lynx, pine marten, and wolverine.

Less primitive recreational opportunities include motorcycle trails, snowmobile trails, lakes with boat launches, interpretive trails, fishing derbies, and scenic drives. Thirty-two campgrounds on the Colville National Forest provide a wide array of overnight stays, from lakeside developed camps to wide spots on logging roads way back in the woods.

The 49 Degrees North Ski Area, near the town of Chewelah, operates privately on national forest land under a special permit. Billed as a comfortable, family ski area, it offers several chairlifts and more than twenty ski runs. Cross-country ski and mountain bike trails near here provide alternatives to downhill skiing.

Interpretive trails near Sullivan Lake and Kettle Falls tell the story of early logging, sawmilling, and mining on the Colville National Forest. Signs at an archaeological dig at Pioneer Park Campground on the Pend Oreille River describe early Indian life. An interpretive exhibit set among burned-out snags along Washington Highway 20 near Sherman Pass dramatizes and explains the White Mountain Fire of 1988.

The Sherman Pass National Forest Scenic Byway on Highway 20 between Republic and Kettle Falls is the most well-known of the many scenic drives on the Colville National Forest. From this twisting mountain highway visitors can see why this area is so special.

Few other cars distract drivers from the views on either side. From Sherman Pass, at the high point of the

Grizzly bears have a somewhat exaggerated reputation for size and ferocity. Although they may weigh half a ton, they prefer to avoid trouble by steering clear of human activity. They primarily eat grasses, berries, and roots.
TOM AND PAT LEESON

SAVING SPECIAL SPECIES

Wildlife listings make the Colville National Forest sound like Alaska: caribou, moose, wolf, lemming, grizzly bear. The northeastern corner of the Colville National Forest seems, in some ways, like a little piece of the arctic.

The U.S. Fish and Wildlife Service lists two threatened species — the grizzly bear and bald eagle — and three endangered species — the caribou, wolf, and peregrine falcon — on the Colville National Forest. The Forest Service cooperates with the Washington and Idaho game departments and the Canadian government to develop and put into effect recovery plans for the grizzly and caribou.

Recovery plans describe areas and ways in which survival for rare or endangered species can be improved. The northeastern portion of the Colville National Forest is within the recovery areas for grizzly and caribou. Here, the Forest Service manages resources to maintain or enhance habitat.

The caribou in the Selkirk Mountains of Washington and Idaho are the last remaining herd in the continental United States. In the late 1980s, only thirty animals remained. Since then, some caribou from similar ecosystems in British Columbia have been transplanted into the Selkirks to increase the numbers and genetic vitality of the herd.

Scientists estimate that ten to twenty grizzlies still roam in the

A caribou munches on vegetation in the Selkirk Mountains. The caribou here are the only remaining herd in the continental United States. Mature caribou can be recognized by their shovel-shaped antlers. The antlers of this young caribou are still covered with summer velvet. JERRY PAVIA

Selkirks. Wildlife managers do not plan to import grizzlies from other areas to supplement the population. Instead, they believe the population should increase to a viable level if the bears are protected from human intrusion and appropriate habitat is maintained.

Grizzlies need to be left alone, and the Forest Service helps maintain their solitude by limiting road access within the grizzly recovery area. Roads built for timber harvest are kept to a minimum, and when harvest is finished, the roads are closed. Because grizzlies eat a wide variety of foods and adapt to many different ecosystems, their needs for seasonal food supply and cover demand little special resource management. However, high-elevation, north-facing slopes are preserved for winter grizzly dens.

Caribou need very specific ecosystems at different times during the year. In the spring, they range through open forests at mid-elevations, *feeding on young, green plants. They spend the summer and fall in high-elevation basins, forested by subalpine fir and spruce, where they feed on shrubs and grasses. In early winter, they again descend to mid-elevations, where the old-growth cedar and hemlock woods provide shelter from the deepening snows.*

As the winter snow settles and firms so the caribou can walk on top with their large, snowshoe-like feet, the animals move back up to high elevations, where they feed on beard lichens that hang from subalpine trees. The caribou can reach lichens high in the branches because they are standing on six to ten feet of snow. When calving time approaches in the spring, the pregnant cows leave the herd and go up to the ridgetops, away from predators, to give birth.

Managing an area for caribou is complex. Several different ecosystems must be identified and protected, each in the appropriate season. Caribou habitat management takes up many pages in the Colville National Forest plan, which limits timber harvest and recreation activities in critical caribou habitats.

If caribou and grizzly populations increase in the coming years, credit will be given to careful wildlife and habitat management in the recovery areas. Future visitors to the Colville National Forest may then be more likely to catch sight of a caribou herd grazing on a mountainside or a grizzly crashing through the underbrush. If so, the Forest Service and cooperating state and federal agencies will have helped two species in the United States come back from the edge of extinction.

The male ruffed grouse beats its wings, making a muffled thumping sound that suggests a distant motor starting up. Ruffed grouse nest in sheltered depressions on the forest floor and lay from eight to fourteen buff-colored eggs. TOM AND PAT LEESON

drive, a short trail leads to viewpoints. Other short stops include the Log Flume Interpretive Trail, a half-mile flat walk among the ruins of a logging operation from the 1920s, and the White Mountain Fire interpretive signs. For those with more time, Canyon Creek and Sherman Pass campgrounds offer rustic campsites with water, tables, pit toilets, and small fees.

When General Sherman of Civil War fame crossed the Kettle River Range in the 1860s, he probably never imagined that a paved highway bearing his name would curve through these mountains to connect northeast Washington with the Idaho Panhandle. Yet it's easy for visitors to turn their backs to the road, look out over the mountains cresting in all directions, and feel the wildness he must have experienced. The Colville National Forest has not been entirely tamed into an urban playground like some national forests closer to large cities.

The northeastern part of Washington is often called "the forgotten corner" of the state. Those who have discovered the memorable wildness, beauty, and rich history of the Colville National Forest may want to change the nickname. Perhaps "the unforgettable corner" is more appropriate. ■

The Mill Pond Interpretive Trail near Sullivan Lake is barrier-free, allowing visitors with a wide variety of abilities to tour the easy mile-long loop. The bridge spans the top of the modern concrete dam, located in the same spot as the 1910 wooden structure that first created the historic millpond.
MIKE JAVORKA

COLVILLE
NATIONAL FOREST DIRECTORY

POINTS OF INTEREST

LITTLE PEND OREILLE RECREATION AREA is a system of trails suited to a variety of recreational needs along Tiger Highway, between Colville and Ione, including cross-country skiing, hiking, camping, and picnicking. Off-road vehicle trails are nearby, and small lakes offer boating, sailing, fishing, and swimming.

NOISY CREEK MOUNTAIN SHEEP FEEDING STATION at the base of Hall Mountain near Sullivan Lake provides close views of bighorn sheep. The best viewing is in December or January.

THIRTEEN MILE ROADLESS AREA offers remote, backcountry opportunities in steep, rocky, pine-covered terrain.

WILDERNESSES

SALMO-PRIEST 30,100 acres on the Colville include old-growth cedar and hemlock forests and treeless, alpine cliffs. Home to grizzly bear and caribou.

RECREATIONAL OPPORTUNITIES

HIKING AND RIDING About 400 miles of trails access the Kettle Crest, Abercrombie-Hooknose, Thirteen-Mile, and Selkirk Mountains. The ten-mile Stage Trail, an old wagon trail between Albian Hill and Lambert Creek, connects to the the Kettle Crest National Recreation Trail.

CAMPING Twenty-three campgrounds for tents, recreational vehicles, and trailers. Dispersed camping is allowed in most of the national forest.

SCENIC DRIVES The Sherman Pass Scenic Byway, between Republic and Kettle Falls on Washington Highway 20, offers breathtaking views and provides access to numerous recreational trails and sites. The byway showcases the history and culture of Native Americans, wildfires, early settlers, mining, and forest management.

HUNTING White-tailed deer, elk, moose, and mountain sheep. Deer hunting especially popular because of the large population.

FISHING Cutthroat, rainbow, German brown, and eastern brook trout populate many high country lakes and streams. Lake Roosevelt also contains walleye, sturgeon, and kokanee salmon.

ALPINE SKIING The 49 Degrees North Ski Area (four chairlifts) at Chewelah Mountain has a variety of runs on its 1,845 vertical feet of slopes.

CROSS-COUNTRY SKIING Sixty miles of marked and groomed cross-country ski trails. The most popular trails are Nelson-Calispell, Boulder-Deer Creek Summit, Frater Lake, and Geophysical.

SNOWMOBILING More than 300 miles of signed trails including Lake Butte-Kelly Mountain, Chewelah Mountain-Power Peak, Paupac-LeClerc Creek, and Quartz Mountain-Eagle Rock.

OFF-ROAD VEHICLES Three areas — Batey-Bould, Little Pend Oreille, and Taylor Ridge-Twin Sisters — have trails for trail bikes and four-wheel drives. All roads and trails in the national forest are open to off-road vehicles unless posted otherwise.

ADMINISTRATIVE OFFICES

FOREST HEADQUARTERS 695 South Main, Colville, WA 99114 (509) 684-3711

COLVILLE RANGER STATION 775 South Main, Colville, WA 99114 (509) 684-4557

KETTLE FALLS RANGER STATION 255 West 11th, Kettle Falls, WA 99141 (509) 738-6111

NEWPORT RANGER STATION 315 North Warren, P.O. Box 770, Newport, WA 99156 (509) 447-3129

REPUBLIC RANGER STATION 180 North Jefferson, P.O. Box 468, Republic, WA 99166 (509) 775-3305

SULLIVAN LAKE RANGER STATION Metaline Falls, WA 99153 (509) 446-2681

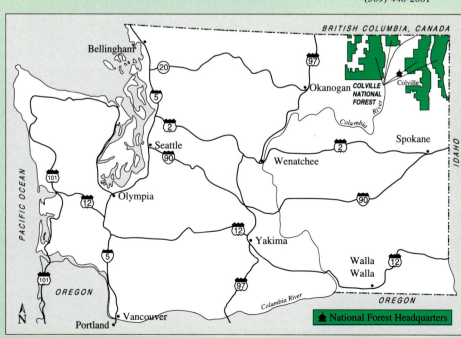

Granite Creek slides down through a sinuous trough in bedrock and then cascades over a fifty-foot cliff to form Granite Falls. The falls is one of the highlights of exploring the back roads of the Priest Lake Ranger District on the Kaniksu National Forest. U.S. FOREST SERVICE

Kaniksu
NATIONAL FOREST

Small in area, big in rewards

Washington, Idaho, and Montana share the rocky crags, huckleberry fields, and vigorous forests of the Kaniksu National Forest, one of the three forests making up the Idaho Panhandle National Forests. In Washington, western hemlock, western white pine, Douglas-fir, western larch and western redcedar thrive in the wet, mild climate and rich volcanic soils of the west slopes of the Selkirk Mountains.

The Priest Lake Ranger District of the Kaniksu National Forest manages 125,000 acres in the northeastern corner of Washington. The Colville National Forest administers another 150,000 acres of the national forest in Washington state.

Whether you drive from Sullivan Lake in Washington or Priest Lake in Idaho, it's a long trip on gravel roads to the Roosevelt Grove of Ancient Cedars. But the trees are worth the time and trouble. Named after President Theodore Roosevelt, an avid outdoorsman, the grove was first set aside in the early 1900s and designated a scenic area in 1943. Some of these shaggy redcedars sprouted during the Middle Ages and have been growing for more than 1,000 years. The biggest trees are ten feet in diameter and 150 feet tall.

Fire has swept past this grove many times, repeatedly devastating surrounding woods. Between

1900 and 1930, more than 50 percent of the Kaniksu National Forest burned. The cedars escaped the flames because they are rooted in wet, boggy ground near Granite Creek. The worst recent fire, in 1926, burned some of the grove, but seventy acres of the big trees still stand.

A one-mile trail begins in a small lower grove and climbs along Granite Falls to a larger upper grove before looping back to the trailhead. During low water in late summer, Granite Falls seems to fall sideways as it pours down slanted slabs of granite. When snowmelt swells the creek in the spring, the pounding falls wears holes in the rocks below.

Western hemlock and white pine grow among the redcedar that dominate the upper grove. Queencup beadlily, trillium, and lady fern grow beneath the trees. Wild ginger adds a pungent smell to the air. Red squirrels chatter, and varied thrush trill from the tree branches.

Visitors can spend the night among the giant trees.

Sunlight glows on the shaggy bark of giant western redcedar, left, and Douglas-fir and western hemlock trees. Redcedar can survive on dry sites, but grow best on wet, or even swampy ground. The species has been nicknamed "canoe cedar" because early Indians carved the trunks into giant canoes, some of which measured more than sixty feet in length. RAY ATKESON

Four campsites in the lower grove have tables and vault toilets and there is no fee. The campground is named Stagger Inn, after a fire camp that was built on the site in 1926. Legend has it that firefighters who had to hike the fifteen miles from the town of Nordman could only "stagger in" when they reached camp.

Trees aren't the only attraction in the western Kaniksu National Forest. Petit Lake, a few miles south, and Muskegon Lake, a few miles north of Roosevelt Grove, have vehicle access, campsites near their lakeshores, and rainbow trout in their clear waters. Retreating Ice Age glaciers created these shallow lakes by leaving behind ice chunks the size of city blocks. These stranded icebergs melted and filled their holes with water.

Huff Lake, a boggy lake just off the road into Roosevelt Grove, grows several species of sensitive plants. Bog cranberries ripen each summer. The lake even hosts carnivorous plants. Small sundews with their round leaves, for example, look innocent enough. But when insects land on their sticky leaves, long hairs slowly bend inward to trap the prey. Then the sundews digest the insects through the leaves.

Huckleberries grow so thickly on the Kaniksu National Forest that commercial pickers join recreational pickers to harvest them each year. Especially good huckleberry fields can be found east of Newport.

The Kanisku provides, as well, timber for wood products and water used in the Spokane area. Cattle, horses, and goats also graze on national forest lands.

Hunters stalk deer and elk in the Washington portion of the Kaniksu each fall. Special seasons in some areas allow bow hunters and muzzleloader hunters to practice their skills. The national forest also boasts one

Huckleberries come in blue, purplish black, and ruby red. The high-elevation species grow close to the ground for protection from wind and cold. The lower-elevation varieties grow into bushes. MIKE JAVORKA

Round-leaved sundews usually grow in peat bogs. The flowers are small, rarely exceeding one-eighth of an inch in diameter, and are usually closed, opening for only a short time in the middle of the day. Old herbal texts recommended elixir of sundew as a cure for consumption or to remove warts or corns.
JOHN SHAW/TOM STACK AND ASSOCIATES

The North American moose, above, is the largest deer in the world. Bull moose can weigh 1,500 pounds and stand six feet high at the shoulder. Bull moose antlers are covered with nourishing velvet until late summer, when it peels off. HARRY ENGELS

Hikers in the Salmo-Priest Wilderness can look northwest from Shedroof Divide, above, and gaze upon the sea of Selkirk Mountains in the northeast corner of Washington.
U.S. FOREST SERVICE

of the only areas in Washington where hunters get a once-in-a-lifetime chance to bag a moose.

Other big game can be found here, but these species are protected from hunting. A few remaining grizzly bear and wolves roam the Kaniksu National Forest. The secretive grizzlies inhabit the dense forests and open brush fields common throughout the Selkirk Mountains, a range that is also home to the last remaining herd of woodland caribou in the continental United States.

The woodland caribou and wolf are listed as endangered species by the U.S. Fish and Wildlife Service, while the grizzly is a threatened species. The Kaniksu National Forest is cooperating with British Columbia, Washington, and Idaho to develop recovery plans for these rare animals.

Areas with minimal road access are set aside for the grizzly to maintain the privacy the big bears require, but no new bears are being brought into the area. The caribou herd, on the other hand, is being enlarged with animals imported from Canada. Foresters also are preserving caribou winter range in old-growth forests and summer range in open areas when planning timber harvests.

The Shedroof Divide in the Salmo-Priest Wilderness offers views west into Washington and east into Idaho. The Shedroof National Recreation Trail travels along a ridgetop that forms the boundary between the Kaniksu and Colville national forests. Hikers stroll through open beargrass meadows and subalpine forests, where they may glimpse a bear, moose, or caribou. Few people visit this wilderness, so solitude is easy to find.

The Washington portion of the Kaniksu National Forest is relatively uncrowded. It is tucked away from population centers, so few people from outside the local area know of its beauty and its recreational opportunities. Almost half its visitors come from Spokane and most of the rest from Idaho. This little piece of a national forest may be small and undiscovered, but it grows big trees, hosts big game, and offers big rewards for those who explore it. ■

KANIKSU
NATIONAL FOREST DIRECTORY

POINTS OF INTEREST

PRIEST LAKE MUSEUM AND VISITOR CENTER opened in 1990 with information and displays about the Priest Lake, Idaho, area and the Kaniksu National Forest. Local history, natural geological processes, and Forest Service management are depicted in photos, text, and exhibits. Located at Luby Bay, just north of Hills Resort, adjacent to Priest Lake.

ROOSEVELT GROVE OF ANCIENT CEDARS is located eleven miles north of Nordman, Idaho. The grove was set aside in 1943 to preserve a virgin cedar forest with trees twelve to forty feet in diameter. Some trees in the grove are more than 1,000 years old. A nature trail passes through an upper and lower grove.

GRANITE FALLS, adjacent to the Roosevelt Grove of Ancient Cedars, is a spectacular sloping falls that gushes over solid granite. The overlook trail goes above the falls for a dramatic view from a sheer cliff face.

WILDERNESSES

SALMO-PRIEST 9,940 acres containing scenic views of the Selkirk Mountains. Home to the only known population of woodland caribou in the continental United States and to the threatened grizzly bear.

RECREATIONAL OPPORTUNITIES

HIKING AND RIDING Sixty miles of trails on the Washington portion of the Kaniksu include the Salmo Loop National Recreation Trail near the Canadian border that accesses high country between Priest Lake and Pend Oreille River drainages.

CAMPING Stagger Inn Campground, located at the Roosevelt Grove of Ancient Cedars, has four developed sites. Dispersed campsites at Petit and Muskegon lakes. Camping is allowed in most areas of the national forest.

LOOKOUTS Two lookouts are staffed throughout the summer and welcome visitors. Indian Mountain, located off the Nordman-Metaline Road, and South Baldy, off the Kings Lake Road, offer spectacular views.

SCENIC DRIVES Pass Creek Pass, connecting Nordman, Idaho, with Metaline Falls, Washington. Not suitable for vehicles pulling trailers. Check road conditions before traveling.

HUNTING Moose, white-tailed deer, black bear, cougar, elk, and grouse. Trapping for bobcat, pine marten, beaver, and mink is also available.

FISHING Streams flowing into Priest Lake are generally closed to fishing to protect spawning cutthroat and bull trout. Small lakes, including Muskegon and Petit, are open and stocked on a regular basis.

CROSS-COUNTRY SKIING Mountain Meadows guest ranch, with miles of marked trails on the national forest, is located in the lower West Branch of the Priest River.

SNOWMOBILING Thirty miles of marked and groomed trails are located in the South Baldy and Pyramid Pass areas. Trails are accessed from the Pend Oreille River Road. Granite Falls is a popular winter destination in the northern part of the national forest.

OFF-ROAD VEHICLES Travel allowed on national forest roads.

ADMINISTRATIVE OFFICES

FOREST HEADQUARTERS Idaho Panhandle National Forests include the Kaniksu National Forest, 1201 Ironwood, Coeur d'Alene, Idaho 83814 (208) 765-7223

PRIEST LAKE RANGER STATION HCR 5, Box 207, Priest River, Idaho 83856 (208) 443-2512

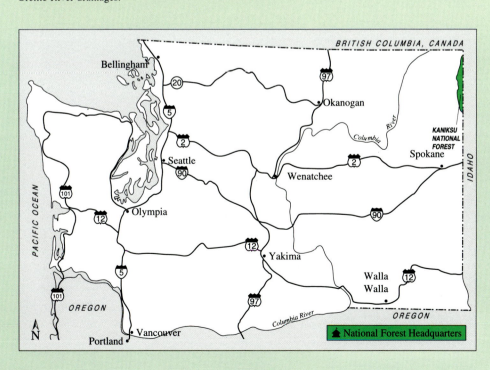

The rich yellow-green needles of ponderosa pine are known for reflecting sunlight in a particularly shimmering way. This pine in the Wenaha-Tucannon Wilderness of the Umatilla National Forest proves the point. The thick rust-colored bark and tall straight trunks of ponderosa are frequent visual rewards for national forest visitors. PAT O'HARA

Umatilla
NATIONAL FOREST

Far from the madding crowds

The Umatilla National Forest, in the Blue Mountains of southeastern Washington and northeastern Oregon, encompasses a series of lava plateaus cut by stream canyons. And much of the national forest's 300,000 acres in Washington lies within the 177,465-acre Wenaha-Tucannon Wilderness.

Hikers and horseback riders descend into steep-sided canyons in the Wenaha-Tucannon Wilderness, in contrast to hikers in other Washington wildernesses who climb to the mountaintops. Because the Wenaha-Tucannon Wilderness reverses the pattern, it has been called "the upside-down wilderness."

Like all national forest wildernesses, the Wenaha-Tucannon is closed to motorized vehicles and equipment. Forest Service trail crews use mules and horses to pack in cross-cut saws and other hand tools. During their working campouts, they maintain wilderness trails the old-fashioned way, with muscle power.

Hunters account for much of the recreation use in the national forest. One of the largest Rocky Mountain elk populations in the United States roams the Umatilla National Forest. More than 20,000 of these 600-pound herbivores graze in open areas on the national forest during the summer before migrating to lower elevations for the winter.

Tens of thousands of hunters come to the

Rocky Mountain elk, left, are a highly adaptable species, able to graze on grasses or browse on shrubs. During the summer, they are most commonly found in open areas where forage is best. A mature bull can weigh 1,000 pounds, with antlers alone weighing twenty pounds.
DON ERICKSON

These vibrant yellow blossoms, below left, are members of the sunflower family. Each flower is actually made up of many small flowers joined together. The sunflowers are the largest of the Washington wildflower groups.
LIGHTBULB WINDERS

Washington portion of the Umatilla National Forest each fall to hunt deer and elk, sometimes traveling up to fifteen miles into the wilderness on horses. They set up camps here and stay out for more than a week. Some local hunting families have been using the same camping spots for three generations.

The national forest is also home to grouse, black bear, and bighorn sheep. Bighorn sheep were native to the Blue Mountains, but hunting eliminated them early in the twentieth century. State wildlife departments have transplanted Rocky Mountain bighorn and California bighorn to the national forest, in hopes of rebuilding the herd. A few hunters with bighorn permits stalk the curly-horned beasts each fall.

Recreation opportunities also include camping, picnicking, hiking, horseback riding, fishing, mushroom gathering, berry picking, and winter sports such as cross-country skiing and snowmobiling. Ski Bluewood, a downhill ski area in the national forest east of Walla Walla, offers an uncrowded alternative to bustling ski slopes closer to urban areas.

The Indian name "Umatilla" probably means "water rippling over sand," and the clear, clean water in the streams and rivers of the Umatilla National Forest supports that translation. The Mill Creek drainage on the northwestern side of the national forest supplies more than eight million gallons of high-quality domestic water each day to the city of Walla Walla.

Salmon hatch in national forest streams, migrate to the ocean via the Columbia River, and then return to the national forest to spawn. Trout and other fish also

Ski Bluewood, above, leases national forest land to run a commercial ski area on slopes just west of the Wenaha-Tucannon Wilderness. The chairlifts and downhill runs are an easy drive from the city of Walla Walla.
EARLE ROTHER

swim in the clear waters. Forest Service fisheries biologists are enhancing fish habitat on the national forest through such projects as log weirs that slow streamflow and create pools for resting and spawning fish.

The Nez Perce, Cayuse, Palouse, Walla Walla, and Umatilla Indians have found food, shelter, and spiritual renewal in the Blue Mountains for thousands of years. Some continue to use the Umatilla National Forest today for such traditional activities as fishing, hunting, gathering, and religious purposes.

The national forest supports 201 species of birds, seventy-three species of mammals, twenty-nine species of fish, fourteen species of reptiles, and seven species of amphibians. Seventy-five percent of these species depend on habitat along streams and rivers. Other important habitat areas include meadows and old-growth forests.

The national forest produces enough timber annually to build more than 70,000 homes. Most of the trees harvested are ponderosa pine, Douglas-fir, grand fir, and western larch. Partial cutting is increasingly replacing clearcutting as the preferred method of harvest, in order to help maintain wildlife habitat and ecosystem health and diversity.

Grazing has been a primary use of the national forest since 1860. The 10,000 cattle and 8,000 sheep that

Layers of basalt rock peek through vegetation on the steep valley sides of Asotin Creek, left, in the 10,416-acre Asotin Wildlife Recreation Area. Runny basaltic lava welled up from fissures in the earth many times fifteen million years ago and spread like water over most of southeastern Washington and northeastern Oregon. BOB AND IRA SPRING

graze today on one million acres of grazing allotments represent only a fraction of the large herds that historically used the national forest for summer range.

Other resource harvests on the national forest include the gathering of berries, mushrooms, firewood, and yew bark. Pacific yew is a short, unimpressive tree with gray bark, usually left behind after timber harvest. Until recently it was not seen as a commerical product.

But scientists have discovered that yew bark contains a chemical called taxol that shows promise as a cancer treatment. Forest managers are mapping the distribution of Pacific yew on the national forest and evaluating its ecological role. Eventually it may be cultivated and harvested commercially for medical reasons.

The Washington portion of the Umatilla National Forest occupies a unique niche in any tally of resources and opportunities in Washington's national forests. Located far from any other national forest in the state, it is warmer and drier and hosts different combinations of plants and animals. It has the most lava flows, due to its location along one of the largest extrusions of lava in the world. It has the most elk, the fewest redcedar, and the lowest levels of precipitation. And it is the only national forest in Washington with a wilderness turned upside down. ∎

Hikers walk along the steep slopes above the Wenaha River, in the Umatilla National Forest. The Umatilla contains many secluded spots for recreationists who want to enjoy the outdoors in solitude. DON ERICKSON

UMATILLA
NATIONAL FOREST DIRECTORY

POINTS OF INTEREST

CLEARWATER LOOKOUT/HELIPORT, built in 1935, is a 99-foot tower offering a bird's-eye view of the Wenaha-Tucannon Wilderness.

KENDALL SKYLINE ROAD offers spectacular views of the area. It started as a private road prior to World War I, was completed by the Civilian Conservation Corps in 1930, and dedicated in 1950.

WILDERNESSES

WENAHA-TUCANNON 177,465 acres of deep canyons and steep sideslopes of the Wenaha and Tucannon rivers. Elevations range from 2,000 to 6,400 feet. The wilderness straddles the Washington-Oregon border and is a popular area for hunters, anglers, and backpackers.

RECREATIONAL ACTIVITIES

HIKING AND RIDING More than 300 miles of trails for the hiker, backpacker, and horseback rider. The trails offer a variety of difficulty levels. Check with national forest offices for specific trail information.

CAMPING is available throughout the national forest, and six developed campgrounds are maintained by the Forest Service. Check with national forest offices for availability and accessibility information.

SCENIC DRIVES Forest Road 40 begins fifteen miles south of Pomeroy, Washington, off County Road 128 and travels along ridgetops with panoramic views of the Blue Mountains, the Wenaha-Tucannon Wilderness, the Eagle Cap and Wallowa mountains in Oregon, and the Seven Devils in Idaho. The Kendall Skyline Road starts in Dayton, Washington, on Forest Road 64 and offers spectacular vistas of canyons, mountains, timber, and the Columbia River. Routes are closed in the winter.

WHITEWATER RAFTING AND KAYAKING The Grande Ronde River does not require a permit for individuals or private groups. Outfitters, guides, and shuttle services are available.

HUNTING White-tailed and mule deer, Rocky Mountain elk, bighorn sheep, black bear, and mountain lion. Washington hunting license required.

FISHING Good fishing on the Grande Ronde, Wenaha, Tucannon, and Touchet rivers and their tributaries. Fish include steelhead, rainbow, and Dolly Varden trout, and chinook salmon. Washington fishing license required.

ALPINE SKIING Ski Bluewood (two chairlifts and one platter pull), twenty-one miles southeast of Dayton, Washington, has twenty-six runs. A day lodge, ski equipment rental, and ski school are available. Sno-park permits are required and are available at the lodge.

CROSS-COUNTRY SKIING Opportunities on most backcountry roads. Access to snow-plowed state highway turnouts is provided through Washington Sno-park permits, available at the Washington State Parks and Recreation Commission.

OFF-ROAD VEHICLES Opportunities are found on many miles of forest roads.

SNOWMOBILING Forest roads and more than 100 miles of groomed trails centered around Mount Misery and Touchet.

ADMINISTRATIVE OFFICES

FOREST HEADQUARTERS 2517 Southwest Hailey Ave., Pendleton, OR 97801 (503) 276-3811

POMEROY RANGER STATION Rt. 1, Box 53-F, Pomeroy, WA 99347 (509) 843-1891

WALLA WALLA RANGER STATION 1415 West Rose Street, Walla Walla, WA 99362 (509) 522-6290

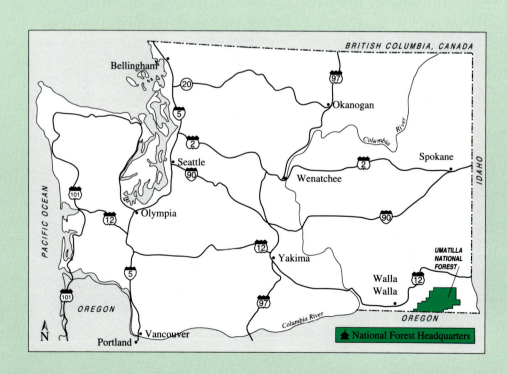

Evening light silhouettes a lone tree on the Mount Baker-Snoqualmie National Forest. PAT O'HARA

Conclusion

NATIONAL FORESTS

Meeting regional and national needs

The poet Robert Frost once asked, "Whose woods are these?" His question has been repeated over and over again during the hundred years since Congress created the national forests. In the final two decades of the twentieth century, the question of who owns the national forests of Washington became the focus of an intense national debate.

In the early part of the twentieth century, people living near the national forests viewed them as local, or even personal, assets. Nearby residents were accustomed to taking what they needed from government land. It took decades before Forest Service controls on such matters as timber harvest and grazing were readily accepted.

During most of the twentieth century, the national forests were a regional resource, providing a steady flow of timber and other resources to create and sustain state and local economies. Loggers and mill workers, for example, directly depended on timber harvest for their livelihood. Funds from timber sales supported schools, roads, and other services throughout Washington.

The regional claim to national forest resources went largely unchallenged until the 1980s, when national environmental groups began lobbying to limit harvest of old-growth forests. They argued that most of the once-vast woods of the Pacific Northwest had been cut and that the remaining old trees should be

MILK COW TO MOTORHOME

Harold Engles outlived the paper clip on the pages of his Forest Service field diaries from the early 1920s. The paper clip had rusted away by the 1990s, while Harold was still striding about the mountains with his friends in the "Over 70 Hiking Club."

Harold was sixteen years old when he joined the Forest Service in 1919, only fourteen years after the agency began. He knew Gifford Pinchot, the first chief of the Forest Service, and Bob Marshall, one of the early advocates of wilderness areas. Engles worked for the Forest Service for more than thirty years and remained active as an adviser and volunteer for more than thirty years after his retirement. He helped create the history of the national forests of Washington.

In 1927, he came to Darrington, Washington, as the district ranger of the Darrington Ranger District of the Snoqualmie National Forest. The district had only two employees back then — a forester in charge of timber sales and Harold, who was in charge of everything else, including administration, blacksmithing, and secretarial services. They worked out of a small, unfinished ranger station with no electricity. The only vehicle parked outside was a wagon with a team of mules.

Harold Engles, who has seen the Forest Service evolve over several decades, walks in the woods outside his home near Darrington. CLIFF LEIGHT

"Today they must have sixty full-time employees at the Darrington ranger station," Harold said when asked to compare the Forest Service of 1927 to that of the 1990s. "If I had included all the mules and horses in the district, I still wouldn't have had that number."

Engles spent most of his time in the field, locating trail, supervising lookout construction, and fighting fires. Hikes of forty-five miles in one day were commonplace, and Harold thought nothing of carrying a 100-pound pack and spending nights out under a boulder or a fallen tree. It was part of the job, and he loved it.

To Engles, nothing was impossible, and he often proved it. He decided a fire lookout could be built on the south spire of 6,800-foot Three Fingers Mountain, and he built one. His crew blasted the top fifteen feet off the peak to leave a square platform that just held the box cabin. Anything heaved off the east side of that platform fell 2,500 feet to the valley below. One worker that marched off the job in disgust said, "I ain't no eagle, and I didn't hire out to be no eagle."

Mules carried the materials for building the lookout up the mountain and across a glacier to the base of the rock pyramid of the summit. There, the supplies were winched up the last 600 feet. When the lookout was completed in 1932, no one could walk all the way around it because it hung over the edges of the flat mountaintop on two sides.

The Forest Service of today is a far different organization from the

preserved to provide wildlife habitat, a bank of genetic diversity, stabilization for the global climate, and undisturbed ecosystems for human appreciation.

Are these stands of mature trees a national treasure or a regional crop? The debate over this question became headline news all over the United States in the 1980s and 1990s. The argument reached into courtrooms, as groups filed suits and counter suits. The issue engaged Congress in protracted battles over legislation to limit timber harvest. Environmentalists protested by sitting in trees scheduled for harvest. Timber workers publicized their concerns by driving

one Harold Engles signed on with in 1919. The era of epic projects like the Three Fingers lookout are past. Today's Forest Service district rangers are more likely to spend their days at a desk than on a mountaintop.

At the age of eighty-eight, Harold sat in his rocking chair in his Darrington home and talked about changes in the Forest Service during his lifetime.

"I go to Forest Service meetings today, and it boggles my mind," he said. "I think one of the biggest changes I've seen is the intensive study that goes into timber sales. They cover so may angles — soil testing, the effect on wildlife and fisheries. Everything seems to be carefully considered and interwoven into one large plan."

When asked how national forests have changed during the more than seventy years he has known them, Harold merely told a story. He had recently been driving on the highway and passed a large motorhome towing a little car. As he looked at the bicycles and other paraphernalia strapped to the huge recreational vehicle, a memory popped into his mind.

He was out hiking in a national forest in 1919 when he heard a terrible clanging noise. Around a curve in the trail came a family: mother, father, kids, and a milk cow. The cow was packed up with all the

The Three Fingers lookout perches precariously atop Three Fingers Mountain. The rocky peaks of the mountain dwarf the lookout, which can be seen in the top right portion of this photo. MAC BATES

gear they needed for a week or two of fishing in the mountains. The kettle and frying pan were bouncing around, banging into each other, making the racket. Not only was that cow a pack animal, she gave fresh milk twice a day to boot.

Harold didn't spell out the moral of the story. He just described the motorhome and the milk cow and left value judgments to his listeners. But there was a bit of wistfulness in his voice when he spoke of the simplicity and challenges of the early days of the national forests.

logging trucks through Washington, D.C.

There is an easy answer to the ownership question. The people of the United States hold title to these public lands. But that answer doesn't solve all the issues raised over land use. The question of what the people want for their national forests will be answered by public opinion, the courts, and legislation. The new balance between regional and national agendas that emerges will control the fate of Washington national forests as they enter the twenty-first century. ■

HELPING YOUR FAVORITE NATIONAL FOREST

National forests educate as well as entertain. With books, brochures, maps, signs, exhibits, and self-guided trails, each national forest teaches visitors about its natural and cultural history and its resource management activities. What many visitors do not know is that much of this interpretive material comes from private organizations, which exist to support the Forest Service and other agencies.

Interpretive associations are non-profit groups that work closely with the national forests to provide many interpretive services. Through the sale of interpretive materials to visitors, associations are able to fund a variety of projects, including the publication of books and trail guides, acquisition of materials for exhibits and libraries, field seminar programs, and other projects to enhance the visitors' understanding of the national forests.

If you would like to find out more about interpretive association activities in your Pacific Northwest national forests, contact:

Northwest Interpretive Association
83 South King St., Suite 212
Seattle, WA 98104
(206) 553-7958

THE NATIONAL FORESTS OF AMERICA SERIES

The National Forests of America series explores the many attractions of the national forests, area-by-area. Eventually the series will cover the entire national forest system.

Each book has approximately 128 pages packed with campground and trail locations, scenic turnouts, phone numbers, addresses, and a map and directory on each national forest.

And the national forest books are illustrated with color photos from noted outdoor photographers.

Other titles in the series include *California National Forests*, *Montana National Forests*, and *Greater Yellowstone National Forests*. *Southern National Forests* will be available in April 1992.

To order the national forests books or to receive a free catalog of Falcon Press books, call 1-800-582-2665 or write to:

Falcon Press
P.O. Box 1718
Helena, MT 59624